BAREFOOT BOY AND OTHER DRIVEL

BAREFOOT BOY
AND OTHER DRIVEL

Published by Up North Storytellers

BAREFOOT BOY AND OTHER DRIVEL

PETER HUBIN

Published by: Up North Storytellers
N4880 Wind Rd., Spooner, WI 54801

Library of Congress Control No. 2010925978

ISBN NO. 978-0-615-36496-4

Printed in the United States of America
By: White Birch Printing, Inc.
501 W. Beaver Brook Ave., Spooner, WI 54801

The author was a young boy learning about the world in the 1940s. He grew up on a farm in northwestern Wisconsin. There was a major highway passing through it, plus a major railroad track was a short distance away. Schooling started in a country school in this rural countryside with many interesting woods to explore, as well as many lakes and streams nearby. The book is factual and hopefully will give the reader a chuckle or two.

PREFACE

The author was a young, barefoot boy in the 1940s, the decade that also contained World War II, the world wide event that changed everyone's lives. He lived in a marvelous area for a young rambunctious boy. The family lived on a farm in northwestern Wisconsin that had a major United States Highway going through it.

The main railroad in the area ran less than one-half mile away. There were hundreds of acres of forests that all needed to be explored, and numerous lakes and streams to fish or swim in.

There was no television in the area at that time, and the country school was the main focus of the neighborhood. The author tries to take the reader back to a time and place that was far simpler than today. However, simple as it seems, that is the way it was. The book is factual, and is as true as his memory allows. The author had a wonderful childhood and was blessed with wonderful, loving parents. He would not have changed a thing about his youth.

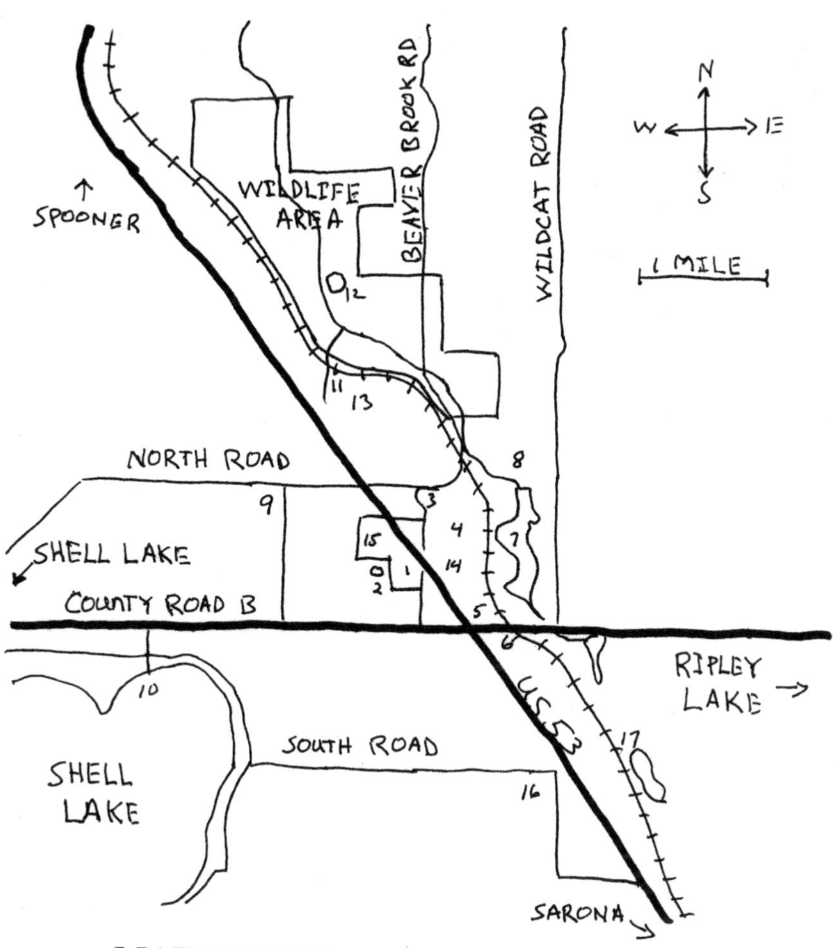

MAP LEGEND OF BEAVER BROOK AS IT WAS IN THE 1940s

1. Home
2. Neighbor's Pond
3. Marsh Hill
4. Humdinger Hill
5. Beaver Brook School - Oscar's Store
6. Railroad Tunnel - Artesian Well - Track Hill
7. Reservoir
8. Cranberry Marsh
9. Betty's Home
10. North Landing
11. Railroad Trestle
12. Beaver Pond
13. Friend's Pasture - Shy Poke
14. Saw-Whet Owl
15. Shrew - Great Horned Owl
16. Fred's Farm
17. Brown's Lake - Hog Nose Snake

BAREFOOT BOY

~~~~~~

Life in the 1940s was far different from today around Shell Lake and northwestern Wisconsin. There were no big box stores, clothing styles were pretty plain and many kids wore bibbed overalls. High fashion had definitely not shown up around rural Shell Lake.

Our shoes and boots were bought at local shoe stores in either Spooner or Shell Lake. Going to the shoe store to buy shoes was cool because one store had a fluoroscope which acted like an x-ray machine. You slid your foot into a small opening in the machine and you could see the all the bones in your foot, plus the outline of the shoe. We would wiggle our toes and we thought it was wonderful to see our own toes. Eventually, someone figured out that the machines may be dangerous, so they disappeared.

The shoes in those days were made out of leather and they were very STIFF. They really needed to be broken in which was very painful. We got blisters on our heels, sore toes, and in general, sore feet. About the time you got your shoes to feel good, because they were finally broken in, you outgrew them. This meant another trip to the shoe store.

Most young kids hated wearing shoes, and as soon as we got warm weather in the spring, and the snow had been gone for a while, we went barefooted whenever we could. When school let out for the summer, our shoes went in the closet. You definitely learned to walk differently outside when you
~~~~~~

were barefoot. It was kind of a shuffling, weight shifting, cautious pace. Most places we walked were not easy to walk on. The roads were alright if you could walk where the car tires ran. By the side of the road you would find a lot of rocks, and they hurt when you stepped on them.

Walking barefoot on hay stubble was really bad. You learned to walk by not lifting your feet, but by sliding them to push over the stubble so it didn't poke your feet. This worked alright until you bumped into a stem from a large plant, such as burdock, bull thistle or Canadian thistle. You could stub your toes on these stubbles and that would hurt big time. Thistles were to be avoided at all cost, as you could get many prickers in your feet.

You quickly learned to avoid any steel, or hard object, that was out in the sun for a few hours. Things like that could get very HOT! Burned feet were really sore feet. Boards with nails in them were bad, too. We built a new barn in 1942, when I was four years old. That summer I stepped on several boards with nails in them. Tetanus shots were given to prevent illness and the shots were probably greatly needed for all the dirt on a barefoot like mine. Some of these nails went very deep in the foot. OUCH!

Something you never avoided were semi-dried up mud puddles, as the thin layer of mud would stick to your feet and it felt great. But the best of all, was stepping in a fresh cow pie. That warm, squishy feeling was the greatest! Cool, fresh cow pies were a close second.

One really nice benefit of going barefoot was that whenever you came to any water, you just went right in. I doubt that any of the kids I knew would ever avoid going in a puddle, stream, pond, swamp or any other form of water or mud. We really loved that feeling of water and mud on our feet. You might have to check for blood suckers when you came out.

One boy I knew told of his Grandpa fishing barefoot in a boat when he caught a snapping turtle. The turtle was in the boat and bit off two of his Grandpa's toes. My Dad told of one of his brothers standing by the big hay rope as they pulled hay up into the barn. He was barefoot and put his toe on the rope as it was being pulled back. He stood by a large pulley that changed the direction of the rope. He made a miscalculation and his toe got pulled into the pulley and his toe was nearly cut off.

Climbing trees was a big deal for us when we were young. We thought it was our duty to climb trees in a yard. Being barefoot really helped us climb up the trees. Tarzan was a comic book hero and he lived in the trees so that was good enough for us. Jumping from branch to branch - forget it! We couldn't do that.

The lawns were very small in the 1940s as power lawn mowers hadn't shown up around our neighborhood. Lawns were mowed with a hand pushed mower and that was hard work. The lawns were quite small because of the hand mowing. Generally, lawns were great places to play barefooted. The soft cool grass was wonderful on our feet.

Among the drawbacks, besides cuts, bruises, puncture wounds, etc., was not being able to walk in the house without some precautions. If my feet weren't clean, I had to take a brush with soap and water to clean them and then dry them. On rare occasions you could come in the house with bare feet without washing them.

Going to Sunday School, or Church, or any special event meant putting on our shoes. Of course, having been barefoot so much of the time, our feet were wider now so our shoes really did not fit.

When I was about age 10 or 11, I gave up and wore shoes all year long. I was really a sight in pictures taken of me in the 1940s, with my bare feet and curly red hair, wearing my bibbed overalls.

In about 1948, a shoe store in Spooner ran a special promotion to sell shoes. The deal was that each pair of shoes, or boots, sold was worth a certain number of points, which could be awarded to any kid the purchaser chose to give them to. For whatever reason, my name was entered and what is even more strange, I got a lot of points! The contest ran for several weeks and a list of the kids and their points was posted and updated. At one point I had the most points of all the kids!

I must have been naïve as I didn't have a clue where these points came from as I did not think anybody knew me. It must have been people that knew my Mom and Dad. In the end, I think I ended up in 3rd place and I won a pair of clamp on roller skates.

These skates were clamped on to the sole of your shoe, or boot, and then tightened up. They actually worked. However, for a kid living on a farm, this prize didn't work very well. I tried the alleyway in the barn, but that didn't work so good. The nearest blacktop road was County Road B, and it was rough. Besides that, those roller skates kicked my butt! I turned my ankles and fell down numerous times. Anyway, it was fun to have won the skates and try to make them work.

THE RESERVOIR

~~~~~~

In about 1905, the Badger Cranberry Company was formed about a one-half mile from our place. In those days, a cranberry bog needed a good supply of water to flood the plants if there was a threat of frost. The bogs are laid out with channels and gates to route the water to the proper bogs.

A reservoir was made to hold water by building a large dam on Beaver Brook, a relatively small spring fed stream. This made a lake of about 60-70 acres. When it was necessary to flood at night, the water was pumped back into the reservoir the next morning. There were some huge pumps and large pipes to get the job done.

Out in the reservoir a few stumps were sticking up with many more under the water. It was a good place to fish and I spent many hours doing that. Northern Pike were very plentiful and we used dare devil spoons to catch them. We caught way more under water stumps than we did fish.

One winter evening, our country school kids were going to hold a skating party on the reservoir. We met at school, walked down the railroad tracks to the reservoir, down a steep bank and out onto the ice. There was no snow and the ice was pretty smooth. Some of the older boys brought some kerosene along to start a fire out of an old stump that was sticking out of the ice. Alas, the boys best efforts failed, so the skating party was called off because of the cold. It was a fun time anyway, even if we had to eat cold hot dogs.
~~~~~~

Thinking back on that event, it was quite a long distance to go on a winter night. Our teacher was with us, and the older kids did a great job of looking out for the little kids, like me.

Today, the reservoir is not there any more, nor is the cranberry marsh. The State of Wisconsin bought it and now it is part of the Beaver Brook Wildlife Area. The plan is to let nature reclaim the land. Whatever grows there will be able to be enjoyed by all.

My Grandparents' property joined the cranberry marsh property, even though the railroad tracks ran between them. Several of my uncles helped build the dikes and beds and it seems strange that after all those years, there is no cranberry marsh. There are, however, many cranberry plants still there.

OSCAR'S STORE

~~~~~~

Oscar's Store was located at the intersection of U. S. Highway 53 (now U. S. 253) and County Road B in Washburn County, in the Township of Beaver Brook, near Shell Lake. The Beaver Brook School was nearby, and I attended that school from 1944 to 1948, when the school was closed. The world was very different then.

Oscar was a kind-hearted old bachelor who chewed a lot of Beechnut tobacco. This store was a natural stopping place on my way home from school, and was a good addition to what I learned in that country school during the day.

The store was a meeting place for people living near by. Grocery shopping was very different than it is today and most neighbors bought some items there. There was no fresh meat or milk, but he did have bologna, canned goods, cheese, ice cream, cigarettes, snoose and more. No beer or alcohol was available and it was not a coffee hang out. It was a small store and Oscar lived in the back.

As a small boy, I was fascinated by some of the people who stopped in the store. Paul was a farmer who had taken his family to the Matanuska Valley in Alaska in 1935, as part of some governmental program. He spun a lot of interesting stories of that faraway place that wasn't for him and his family. He brought his family back to Beaver Brook.

John was a large man, a bachelor with a big beard and white hair. He lived on the Wild Cat Road and walked wherever
~~~~~~

he went. He came to Oscar's Store to buy provisions from time to time. We could see him walk by the school and later he would go home with a big sack of provisions over his shoulder.

John was a mysterious character to me and the other kids. He would be at Oscar's Store from time to time and he would talk to us. He told about catching fish in some secret lake in the big woods where he resided. He told about shooting a bear one time and when he had it hung up and skinned it, it looked just like a man to him. I believe he gave the bear away because it looked so much like a man that he couldn't eat the meat.

A lot of men stopped to buy snoose or cigarettes. Wally stopped in to buy Copenhagen snoose. He would cut it open on the handy cutter on the wall, tap it on his elbow, open it up and put a pinch in his mouth. Boy, that looked cool.

My brothers and I decided we had to try some Copenhagen snoose. We swiped some, at a time when Oscar was not looking. We headed toward home and opened that can of snoose. We all took a small pinch, just like we had seen Wally do. We put it inside our lip, just like Wally. It didn't take long and we were so dizzy we could barely stand up. That stuff was terrible. We threw the box away and hoped to start feeling better soon.

Oscar also sold gasoline at his store. These were the old hand pumps that you pumped the gas into the top chamber, and then put the nozzle into the car and let the gasoline run down by gravity. When you were finished, you went in, you told Oscar how many gallons you got and you paid him for it. I remember you could buy 5 gallons of gasoline for $1.00.

Oscar also made the best ice cream sandwiches. He would take a pint container of ice cream, cut it into three-quarter inch slices and put those slices between two wafers made of the same thing that ice cream cones were made of. This was a real treat!!! We didn't have ice cream very often.

The Beaver Brook School did not have a source of water, so Oscar let us get water from his pump. This pump was located just outside his back door, and we all took turns taking the shot gun can and getting water from Oscar. We might stop in the store to see what was going on before taking the water back to the school. The teacher, or the bigger boys, would pour the water into the bubbler so we could drink it.

Oscar had an outdoor privy. This was painted white inside and out. Those nice white inside walls were too much temptation for privy poets. Most of the graffiti was skillfully done and some of these poems I remember today. Such as:

> The outhouse poet when he dies
> Should have erected to the skies
> A fitting tribute to his wit
> A monument of solid _ _ _ _.
>
> The people who write on outhouse walls
> Should roll their _ _ _ _ in little balls
> And those who read these lines of wit
> Should eat those little balls of _ _ _ _.

Oscar's store is gone now, but we have memories of a different time when the world was much different. One of the persons who made the world different was D. B. Reinhart, who was a salesman for the Rice Lake Grocery Company when I was a kid. He was a real friendly guy who I met a couple times at Oscar's. His mother used to teach at the Beaver Brook School (I did not have her for a teacher, though). Anyway, he eventually bought the Rice Lake Grocery Company. Later, he moved to LaCrosse and established Gateway Foods, Reinhart Foods, Rainbow Stores and others. He was a Shell Lake native and was very generous with civic projects. He paid to get the Beaver Brook School House moved to Shell Lake to become a part of the Washburn County Historical Museum complex there.

Oscar was a kind, crusty old man and was one of the characters from my childhood. His store went the way of a lot of other aspects of life back then. Small farms, small gas stations and a whole way of life has changed leaving us with memories and respect for how things used to be.

THE POND

~~~~~

Our neighbor had a small pond just over the fence from our farm. It was about an acre in size and was a natural attraction to my friends, my brothers and me. This pond was in a cow pasture, so cows used it also. YUCK! It was also loaded with blood suckers.

Like most kids, we were fascinated by water. Even though this water was very dirty, we swam in the pond, threw rocks in it and looked for whatever we could see along the shore.

One day, I was walking along the shore of the pond when all of a sudden a mother killdeer really startled me. She had five babies under her wings and when I approached her, she suddenly flared up her feathers and scolded me. I stopped cold in my tracks as she had scared me big time. The babies scattered and three of them ran to the water and swam away. I was amazed. The other two babies squatted nearby and I eventually could see them, even though they were absolutely still and difficult to see.

I sat down at a distance and watched them. The mother flew over the chicks that were swimming and she eventually got them to come to shore. She coaxed the two that were hiding to follow her over to the three that swam away. This took perhaps an hour and the mother killdeer made a lot of noise, but she certainly looked after her brood.

In recent times, we have had three to five killdeer nests each year on our farm, so I see many little fluff balls running like crazy. I also see many 'my wing is broken - follow me' rituals from the adults, as they try to lead you away from the nest, or their babies.
~~~~~

One particular pair had their nest in front of one of my hay barns and I had no choice but to put the electric fence down and drive past the nest to put hay in the barn. I would drive within three feet of the nest, and the mother or father would not fly away.

When the fence was down one day, about a dozen beef calves moved close to the nest. The mother stood up, flared up her feathers and squawked at the top of her lungs. The calves moved in close and she intensified her defense of the nest, with wings outstretched, tail up and beak just snapping! The calves would try to smell her and she jumped up and pecked them on the nose! What a brave and defiant show of resistance. She would have died rather than let those calves harm her eggs. Several days later, the eggs hatched and now there were four little fluff balls running all over.

Back to the pond. One day we decided we needed a raft. We went to our woods and cut down a small oak tree and then cut it into a log about five feet long. We used an axe so it took some time to do this. We hauled the log to the pond and put it in to see how it would float. It didn't float, but went down to the bottom.

We regrouped and found a Swede saw and cut a poplar, or aspen tree, to make another log, and we tried to float it. It was much better, so we whacked down enough trees to make a raft about five feet by five feet. We got some boards and nails to finish the raft. I don't recall if we ever asked our neighbor if we could put a raft on his pond.

We must have put an anchor on the raft so it would not drift away. We dove off it and were pretty proud of the raft that we built.

One day, my friend and I swam out to the raft and climbed up on it. I dived off and shortly after going in the water, I felt my glasses hit my knee. Drats, I had forgotten to take them off and now they were at the bottom of the pond. We dived and dived, but to no avail. We did not find my glasses.

When I got home, I had to tell Mom and Dad what happened and face the music. Dad thought for awhile and decided he could take a fog lamp from a car and hook it up to a car battery. We could take this to the bottom of the pond and see the lost glasses. We carried the battery fog light get-up to the pond and waded in with the light. We turned it on and could barely see it because the water was so muddy. Needless to say, those glasses are on the bottom of the pond to this day.

This pond was about halfway between my friend's house and mine. We met there often. Just before he moved to Oregon, we met by the pond. We quite often would wrestle and horse around. This particular day, my friend really kicked my butt. I must have been getting too big for my britches.

RIPLEY LAKE

~~~~~

After World War II, the Hubin boys were getting interested in going fishing. We knew very little about it, just like everything else in our limited world. We talked Dad into getting some cane poles, line, hooks, bobbers, etc. We pestered Dad to take us, but he was very busy. Finally, one day in June, before doing the milking, he told us to dig some angle worms.

After the milking was done, we tied the cane poles onto the 1937 Ford and headed to Ripley Lake, a small lake about three miles east of our farm. Boy, were we excited! Dad stopped the car and we walked down a fairly steep bank to the lake. The poles were readied, hooks baited and we began fishing. WOW! Look at that bobber go up and down. We started catching fish - bluegills. We did catch one painted turtle, the only one I can ever remember catching in my life. We let the turtle go.

Finally, it was almost dark so we took our 15-20 bluegills and headed home. We scaled and cleaned those fish, and Mom fried them that night. We were all like little birds waiting around the table to be fed, and finally the first fish were put on the table. None of us kids had ever eaten bluegills, but boy they smelled good so we dug right in. As I write this, I can still imagine how those fish tasted. They were the best that any fish ever tasted in my life. All kids should have an opportunity to fish as we did, to admire the fish and to really enjoy eating them. Today, I am more willing to release fish than eat them. It was a different world back then.
~~~~~

For the next several years, my parents took us several times. They would drop us off and come back to get us later. There were two homemade boats near where we fished. No oars, but there were some boards we could use for oars. Each boat had several cans to bail water out and believe me, those boats leaked! We had NO life jackets in those days, either.

Mom would drop us kids off and we would fish most of an afternoon. We would usually walk home when we were done. By this time, I had a casting rod with a level wind reel on it. Boy, that thing could produce some beautiful backlashes! Ripley Lake had a lot of bass as well as lily pads, downed trees and stumps. It was a real bass haven.

I bought a yellow jitter bug and later a red headed mouse. These were surface plugs and you tried to cast it next to a group of lily pads, sunken trees or a stump. Then you let it lay there for 20-30 seconds and then give it a twitch and bingo! The bass would nail that bait and jump out of the water trying to shake that lure. I caught many bass, about two pounds each, on that lake. One day, my girlfriend and eventually to be my wife, Betty Furchtenicht and her dad, Ernest went fishing on Trader's Lake. I caught a four and one-half pound bass and two more weighing five pounds each. Boy, they jumped all over the place.

About this time, I got a pair of plastic chest waders and got interested in using flies and poppers for bluegills with the fly rod. The south end of Ripley Lake was perfect for this and I really enjoyed fishing this way, putting fish in my bamboo creel. I wish I had that creel today. Its end came as Fred, our half-breed St. Bernard could smell fish in the creel as it lay on the ground. We were busy cleaning the fish, so

Fred proceeded to chew up that beautiful creel. Oh, well, that is the way things happen.

One late summer day, my Mom dropped my two brothers, my friend Jerry and me off at Ripley Lake. We would walk home after fishing. My friend had been with his Dad delivering fuel and he had seen a tackle box, several days before, sitting unattended on Deep Lake. On our way home we would need to detour about one and one-half miles to get to Deep Lake, but we decided to do it.

When we were about halfway to Deep Lake from our intended route, it began to rain - no, it poured! It rained as hard as I have ever seen it rain. Talk about four drowned rats. It rained so hard it hurt and it was not hail. We retreated into the brush beside the road. We were absolutely miserable. After many minutes, we wondered if the end was near.

About this time, we heard a car coming so we edged out closer to the road. It was Mom. Boy, I don't know if I was ever so happy to see her in my life. She came looking for us when it started raining and when she didn't see us on the normal way home, she stopped at one of the neighbors and they told her they had seen some boys go on the road to Deep Lake, so that is how she found us.

I spent many happy hours on that lake, and at that time there was a farm at the north end and only one home. Today, homes are all around the lake.

SNOWBANK

~~~~~

In about 1950, we had very high winds in February, which blew the snow and the road past our house was completely plugged from the drifting snow. Township roads, in those days, were not raised up like today, and brush grew in the ditches. There was little place for the snow plow to push the snow in a winter when we had huge amounts of the stuff.

Also, in those days there were a lot of dairy farms, as most rural residents milked cows on their farms. The milk truck picked up milk cans and in the winter the trucks were equipped with a V-plow. Most of the roads were first opened by mid-morning by these milk trucks, as they needed to get the milk to the creamery at Rice Lake or Cameron.

On the morning after this big storm, the milk truck turned off U. S. Highway 53 (which is now 253) and proceeded south toward our farm. It got about 75 yards from the highway and broke an axle. Next, the Washburn County highway department showed up with a huge Oshkosh truck with a V-plow. It got a little farther, but it gave up and left, as it was unable to open the road.

The highway department then came with a big bulldozer with a V-plow on it. For sure that would easily handle the snow drift which was 7 or 8 feet deep, maybe even more. Low and behold, it also failed after making the cleared road only a few yards longer.

Meanwhile, we kids walked over the drifts and caught the school bus on Highway 53. Also, the wind had blown a lot of the snow off the fields, so the county plowed a road through the field so we could drive across the field to the
~~~~~

highway. The milk truck, and all other traffic to our place, came in on this temporary road for two or three weeks.

Finally, it began to thaw. The Washburn County Highway Department brought a D-2 Caterpillar bulldozer to open the road. Now a D-2 is small, but it went up on top of the snow and began pushing at right angles to the road. Back and forth it went and, after several hours, the operator was able to get the road open. The banks that were pushed up nearly reached the high line wires.

WOW! That was really neat because the snow was rolled up and made a lot of neat caves. The weather turned cold so these nice snow caves lasted for several days. My brothers and I spent many hours playing on the banks and in these caves. The field road was abandoned and life returned to normal - but not for long.

Eventually, all of the snow melted, and because most rural roads at that time were dirt and the roads were not raised, they turned into a big sea of mud. For a two week period in March and early April we had 'mud vacation' at our Shell Lake School. Talk about a lousy time for a vacation. Of course, we had to make up the 10 days missed by going several Saturdays during April and May, plus a few extra days in June.

Shortly after that, our Beaver Brook Township and other townships began a vigorous program to widen and raise the road beds. The town roads today are built to handle big snowy winters. Also, today's equipment is much bigger and better able to handle large amounts of snow.

We did have huge amounts of snow in the late 1940s and early 1950s. Many times we had to get out and push the bus on the way to school or on the way home - where was the liability then? No one thought much about that during those days. Many roads had snow banks so high they were over the top of the school bus. So much for the 'good old days'.

THE HOLLOW

~~~~~

The Shell Lake Schools of the 1940s and the early 1950s were for grades 1-12. No kindergarten was offered. The building was perched on the edge of a big hollow. By today's standards, it was a lousy place for a school building. But for the students of my day, it was a wonderful place for a school. I have often wondered why that location was chosen, however.

Kids love hills and valleys and this was a beauty. Just out the south door of the school was a steep hill which had a level spot halfway down to the hollow. This was our main softball field at recess time. In the winter, it became an ice track for cardboard sliding and sleds. It took awhile, but eventually this slippery path reached all the way to the bottom of the hollow. You could really sail on a piece of cardboard.

The real hollow was much lower and it was where the football field was located. Actually, it was a swamp that got filled in during the depression as a WPA project.

From the school, you could walk east down a flight of stairs to a playground area, which was fairly flat with swings and teeter totters, etc., as our school contained all ages of kids. Then, the final steps down to the field were steep and, about halfway down, there was a landing that led to the concrete bleachers which were north of the stairs. The stairs continued to the bottom of the hill where the football field was located.
~~~~~

In those days, we were allowed to bring our sleds on the school bus and many of us would do that on certain days. We would slide before school, at noon hour and recess, if conditions were good.

Leading down to the football field was a road that ran past the first hollow and circled around and reached the football field. When enough kid traffic packed the snow, this was a great hill to slide on. You really had to watch out for kids walking back up the hill, and crashes in front of you. Once, in the 5th grade, I fell off my sled and slid on my face for a distance. My picture that year shows a half-healed, skinned cheek as a sliding badge.

The real sliding challenge was beside the steep steps down to the football field. If you started at the top and didn't drag your feet, you would hit the flat spot about halfway down and fly through the air for 40-50 feet and land on the flat surface beside the football field. We rarely started from the top, but that jump was a great attraction to us.

The trick was to land on the hill and not on the flat. We would start just about at the landing and gradually work our way up depending on conditions. This was real daredevil work and drew a lot of less foolish spectators. There were numerous crashes.

An event occurred on that hill that burned a lasting memory into the minds of all that witnessed it. Don and Jerry had been given a new sled for Christmas. They had made up their minds that they were going to take off from the top of the steps and not drag their feet. Don was the driver and Jerry hung on to his back. They were like 6th and 4th graders, I guess.

This was going to happen during noon hour so the hill was packed with kids. Speculation ran high! At last, the daring (crazy) duo started from the top with no feet dragging. They hit the flat spot halfway down and off they sailed all the way to the flat of the football field. Upon landing, the sled collapsed and parts went flying, as did Don and Jerry. We erupted in cheers and clapped. They were true to their boast!! The boys did not get hurt and the sled could be fixed.

The hill and steps are still there but I don't think many kids use sleds like we did back then. Besides, there is a cable stretched on poles at the edge of the football field. Now hitting that would be very painful.

The hollow was an absolutely beautiful place to play football. There were many maple trees that turned glorious colors in the fall. But it could get foggy. There was a small artesian well 100 feet or so from the south end of the field and teams filled their water jugs there.

I played and practiced on that field and my strongest memories are of practice, but more specifically at the end of practice. We had to run up this very steep hill and, if we didn't do it fast enough, a coach would send us back down to do it over again. Talk about built in motivation to run fast up that hill.

THE HUMDINGER AND THE PEE-DINGER

~~~~~

Winter time for kids in the 1940s and 1950s meant being outside on skis, sleds or skates. In our neighborhood near Shell Lake, Wisconsin, the kids at the Beaver Brook School got together on the weekends.

Skating had to be early in the winter because, in those days, once the snow got deep our desire to shovel the snow off the ice so we could skate soon disappeared. Plus, by the time we got skates on, our fingers would be so cold we could hardly stand it.

Sliding on a road depended on whether or not the hill was plowed and whether sand had been put on it yet. Skiing could generally be done anytime there was snow. Betty and Patty were our neighbors and there were some spectacular hills in their pasture. They were free of trees and the largest hill we called the 'humdinger'. You could get a long ride that ended near the railroad tracks. There were two natural jumps on it, if you had enough courage. Generally, you only made three to five trips down the hill because it was such a long walk back up. Sometimes the walk was shorter if you wiped out.

About 50 yards away was the 'pee-dinger'. This hill was shorter, but very steep. You could not see the bottom of the hill looking down from the top. This hill was a challenge to all of us. If you made it down, you immediately went up another very steep hill and then a long ride ending very near the railroad tracks.
~~~~~

The older kids would build a jump about two thirds of the way down and it took real courage for the little kids to go over the jump.

There would be kids ranging in age from six to fourteen skiing. The older kids really looked after the little ones. As the afternoon wore on, we got colder and wetter and finally it was time to head for home. Betty and Patty lived nearby and I could go to their house to warm up and then walk the road home. Most of the kids had to go about a half mile south to get home. By late afternoon, most of our hands, toes and faces were **really cold**. We always stayed longer than we should have so we were in real pain from the cold. Getting home meant putting your hands and feet in lukewarm water to warm them up. Many a painful tear was shed as we warmed up.

The skis in those days were mostly homemade. Bindings were a leather strap over your toe and inner tube bands under your toe and around the back of your foot. This worked well when you fell. You just twisted your foot to disconnect the ski. However, when it came time to steer your skis, forget it. That was impossible.

We were basically 'shoos boomers' - we just went down the hill in whatever direction we started. Nothing like the skis and bindings that we have today. They may have been available, but not to the kids of the Beaver Brook School.

Looking back at those long ago days, we really had loads of fun. But, boy, those walks back up the hill were hard.

THRESHING MACHINE

~~~~~

In the 1940s, farmers in our neighborhood raised corn, oats and hay to feed their cows, horses, pigs, chickens and other animals. Most corn was put in silos as silage because ripe corn was a greater gamble than it seems like today. Hay was pretty constant and large amounts were put up. Oats were a grain that could be successfully harvested nearly every year.

When the oats got ripe it would be cut with a grain binder. This made bundles about a foot in diameter tied with twine. These bundles would accumulate on steel fingers and when a sufficient number of bundles was reached, the person riding on the grain binder tripped the load and the bundles fell on the ground.

The oat bundles were then put in shocks. Several bundles would be stood up with two or more bundles put on top to help shed rain. This was a manual job and my recollection of this event was that it was a lousy job - hot, dusty and there were usually thistles in the bundles.

Every neighborhood had a threshing machine and in our neighborhood it was owned by Ernest Furchtenicht. Eventually he would become my father-in-law, but when I was a small boy, I looked at him in awe.

On the day that we were to thresh at our place, we watched the road for the threshing machine. At last 'here it comes', roaring up the road being pulled by a Farmall tractor. It was about the biggest machine I had ever seen, other than a steam locomotive.
~~~~~

Ernie would drive around to the west end of our new barn and line things up. He climbed up and swung the big straw spout around so the straw could be blown into the barn. Next, he backed the machine up and dug shallow holes behind each wheel. He then backed the threshing machine into the holes so it would stay in one place. Next, he unhooked the tractor from the threshing machine. He turned the tractor around and lined it up carefully, so he could stretch the big belt from the thresher to the pulley on the tractor.

By now the other farmers had arrived and had driven out into the oats field. They loaded the now dry oat bundles onto their hay wagons. Ernie let the clutch out on the pulley of the tractor and that huge machine began to vibrate - WOW that was so cool!!!

The loads of bundles were unloaded onto an apron that connected them to a bundle cutter that cut the twine. Straw went into the barn and the oat kernels went into bags at the other end of the machine. Quite a deal. We had a grain bin on one side of the hay mow, so the bags of oats had to be boosted up and dragged to the far end of the bin.

This threshing was really a fascination to me and I probably got in the way. I may have even climbed onto the machine. Finally, Ernie had enough! He picked me up and showed me how the bundle cutter whacked up those bundles and warned me that if I fell in there I would be whacked up, too. I think I finally got the message.

That night, or not long thereafter, our family went to the movie in Spooner. I sat at the end of my family, but not at the end of the row. Lo and behold, who should sit down by me but Ernie! I scrunched down in my seat and apparently I told Ernie, "You're not going to throw me into that threshing machine!" Ernie related this story to me when I was much older.

The expression 'feed a threshing crew' was a very real event when I was a kid. Mom made a feast for the 12-15 neighbors that made up the crew. Of course, there was some competition for good meals. The kids had to eat after the crew was done because there was not enough room for all of them.

One neighbor was an old bachelor by the name of John. He was very bashful and would not come in to eat noon dinner. Instead, he said he had to go home and check on the calves, so off he went walking across country. He lived about a mile from our place, but would be ready to work when the crew went back to work after dinner.

By the early 1950s, combines took place of the threshing machines. This closed the history books on a great tradition on thousands of farms in America.

Silo filling was about the same type of program. Strangely, in the 1940s and early 1950s many neighborhood farmers had both a team of horses and tractors. They used tractors for picking up oat bundles and horses for picking up corn bundles. The field chopper spelled the demise of the silo filler and its crew.

The combine and the field chopper meant there would not be threshing crews or silo filling crews to feed big dinners. This also meant that the need to rely on your neighbor for help was slowly changing. Getting together with the neighbors for big jobs was very important in the 1940s and early 1950s. Building barns was a big event, also. Many of the neighbors assisted with building the barn and big dinners were once again prepared for the workers.

THE ARMY RIFLE

~~~~~

My Dad was in the army during World War I and was stationed at a base in New Jersey. At the end of the war, he observed a huge pile of rifles accumulating at the base. He inquired as to what would happen to them and was told they would be loaded on a barge and taken out in the ocean and thrown into the ocean.

My Dad procured one of those rifles, a 1917 Edestone, bolt action .30-06. He had to cut the forearm off a few inches in order to get it in his footlocker, but it came home with him.

The army rifle was rarely used as my Dad did not hunt at all. My oldest brother went deer hunting once and our neighbor used it once, also for deer hunting. It remained a curiosity for young boys.

As we got older, we pestered Dad to shoot it. He warned about the 'kick' so years went by before I ever shot it. And when I did shoot it, believe me, it did 'kick'!

This was a long gun and had a tip-up sight that had markings up to 1700 yards. Shooting at something 1700 yards away was about a mile, so for all practical purposes that tip-up sight was useless. The gun held seven rounds of ammo and weighed about nine pounds.

When I was in the seventh grade, I wanted to go deer hunting in the worst way. In order to do so, I would have had to hunt with an adult and neither my Dad, nor my older brother, were interested. So all I could do was listen to shots being fired and feel jealous. Maybe next year.
~~~~~

School at Shell Lake was dismissed for the entire deer season in those days. As I recall it, my friend was at our place and we decided to smuggle the army rifle out of the house and go hunting in our pasture. I guess we just wanted to get involved with the deer season. We did not have any deer in our pasture and in the late 1940s, there were very few deer anywhere around home. Many winters of deep snow had taken its toll on the deer.

We managed to get the rifle out of the house alright, and took it to the barn. About this time my Dad unexpectedly returned home and drove right up to the barn. HOLY COW!!! "He must know we have the army rifle!" We quickly hid it under the hay in front of the cows on the south side of the barn. Dad proceeded to walk in front of the south side cows to check something with the water system. We made small talk with Dad and he finally left the water system and walked back in front of the cows and stepped on the gun under the hay. He stopped, looked down at it, and we thought 'we are dog meat now', but he continued on his way. Whew, that was close!

When he left, we picked up the rifle, and proceeded out into the woods. Each of us taking turns carrying the gun. Of course, we didn't see any deer and we were so nervous about returning the rifle to the house that we really couldn't enjoy our adventure.

When I was in the 8th grade, I hunted deer for the first time and used the army rifle. I hunted with my friend along with his Mom and Dad. I did not see a live deer all season.

I still have that army rifle today. The barrel has been shortened, the big sight has been ground off, and the magazine has been reduced to hold six rounds. My Dad and I put a new walnut stock on it, with about twenty coats of hand rubbed finish. It has a scope and it still weighs nine and one-half pounds. I have thought about replacing this rifle, but feel a strong attraction to it after all these years.

THE MARSH HILL

~~~~~

Approximately one-half mile north of my house, near Shell Lake, was a beautiful sliding hill we called the Marsh Hill because this road led to the Badger Cranberry Marsh. It was a town road.

If someone started sliding at the top of the hill they would be facing north. As they went down the hill, they turned northwest to a short flat spot and then turned northeast, and by the time they got to the bottom of the hill they would be going east. About this time, the marsh hill road merged with another town road, so there was always the risk of running into, or under, a car. To my knowledge, no one ever did collide with a car.

Now this hill was a real beauty. Good sliding depended on whether the hill was plowed or not, and if sand had been applied, which was hardly ever done in those days. If a person started at the very top of the hill, you would have to drag your feet if you hoped to reach the bottom, and even then it was probably too fast to make the turn at the bottom. This hill was **steep**.

Many Sunday afternoons found neighborhood kids gathered together to go sliding on this hill. Most of them were students who attended the Beaver Brook School, a country school located nearby. Most everybody walked to the hill, which meant you walked back home after sliding. Like most outdoor things, we always stayed longer than we should have so our hands, feet and faces really got cold.
~~~~~

Going down this hill on a sled was really a thrill. Many crashes occurred, also. It was seldom that anybody got hurt, which was great and made it more enjoyable. The walk back up the hill was long.

The last trip of the day we made a train and would 'crack the whip'. A leader would lie on their sled and hook their toes into the front of the sled behind. This was repeated until all the kids and their sleds were in a chain. Now, the last one or two sleds and riders could get hurt, so care always was taken to keep the little kids from those spots.

When the 'train' was ready, a signal was given and everyone started pushing with their hands and the entire train started down the hill. This was quite a sight as sometimes there could be ten to fifteen sleds in the train. The leader would start swerving down the hill and this caused the whole train to swerve back and forth. The sleds on the back end really flew around and could rarely stay connected after about three swerves, as they generally got flipped up over the snow bank. This put other people at the end of the train and the speed picked up, so more sleds and kids went over the bank. WOW! What fun. Finally, we would call it a day and walk home pulling our sleds.

Once, when I was in high school, one of my brothers and I saw our sleds hanging in the shed and decided to give the hill a try. My brother decided to do a 'belly flop' from the top. What he didn't notice was that the runners of the sled were rusty. He took a run and flopped on the sled, but the runner stopped right there and the sled tipped up, so my brother also tipped up on his face and slid down the hill a short distance. He was greatly surprised, but luckily was not hurt.

In August of 1954, or 1955, we got a six inch rainfall in a very short period of time and the marsh hill got washed out. It was rebuilt and blacktopped with asphalt. This hill regularly gets salted sand spread on it now, so kids nowadays don't get the chance to get the thrills we got so long ago on this hill.

MAKING HAY

~~~~~

Putting up hay at our farm in the 1940s was a job for all of the men folks. I was about six or seven when I started helping.

Hay was cut by Dad driving an old F-14 Farmall tractor with lugs, pulling an old horse drawn mower. This cut five feet at a time and the mower ran by the wheels turning on the ground, so it was ground-driven.

Several days after the hay was cut, it would be dry enough to put up. The tractor was hooked up to the dump rake which required one person to drive the tractor and one person to operate the rake. The rake had many large curved teeth which were also springs. The driver drove across the swaths of hay and the dump rake gathered a certain amount of hay. At the appropriate time, the dump rake operator pushed a pedal with his foot and the rake dumped its load. This continued until the entire field was raked into windrows. Sometimes the rows were very crooked as the operator didn't trip the load at the right time. And if you were seven or eight years old, you could barely reach the pedal.

Once the field was raked in this fashion, the crew started at the end of the windrow and raked it into bunches, or 'hay cocks'. When this was finished, the tractor was hooked up to the hay wagon.

The wagon was pulled up next to these hay cocks and my Dad and older brother would pitch hay on the wagon with pitch forks. Rope slings were put down on the bottom of the
~~~~~

wagon and again periodically as the load was made. At this age, I did not drive the tractor, but my younger brothers and I would be on the load 'tramping' the hay down.

When the load got so high that the hay could not be pitched up, we headed for the barn. The load was stopped underneath the peak of the barn. The big hay door was opened so hay could be pulled up into the barn.

The tractor was unhitched from the wagon and driven to the north west corner of the barn where the big hay rope was. My Dad would be hooking up the slings to the part of the carrier that was pulled down from the main carrier on the track. Next, the signal was given to pull up the sling of hay - up it went until it locked on the carrier and disappeared into the barn. The tractor kept going until Dad tripped the load. He began pulling the carrier back toward the peak and this pulled the big hay rope back, also. Driving the tractor backward and not running over the rope took real concentration.

Eventually, we had to go up into the haymow and mow the hay away. This meant pitching it off to the sides to make room for more hay. And that was a hot, dusty, lousy job!

In the late 1940s, our neighbor got a 'hay loader'. This machine was hooked to the back of the hay wagon and moved hay up onto the wagon. Definitely a huge improvement. No more pitching hay up onto the wagon. It still required two people making the load up on the wagon, and one driving the tractor and trying to follow the dump rake windrows which was a real challenge.

By 1948 or 1949, Dad got a 'side delivery rake' through the local cooperative store. This was the real cat's meow. It was made in Canada and came all unassembled, so we had to put it together which was a huge project, at least it seemed like it to me.

This rake produced a continuous windrow around and around the field. Following this was easier, but going around corners was tricky. By this time, driving the tractor, pulling the wagon to pick up hay, was my main job during haying.

Haying was done during the hottest weather of the summer and we really sweated. One bonus was that Mom made lots of kool-aid and cookies and we could eat and drink about all we wanted.

Quite often Dad would take us to O'Connor's Corners, a public landing on the north shore of Shell Lake, to go swimming. This was a real treat, but most times the water was cold. Today this landing is called the north landing.

Putting up hay was definitely a family affair and even though it was hard work, I have fond memories of those days.

MY FRIEND'S PASTURE

~~~~~

My friend's family had a real cool pasture. It was east of U. S. Highway 53 and west of the railroad tracks that ran from Superior to Eau Claire. Their cows got to the pasture by way of an 'underpass' under the highway.

The pasture was at least one hundred acres and had open spaces, a large field by the railroad tracks, woods and a marsh with a small stream running through it. A trail ran to the large field by the railroad tracks and crossed the little stream.

One summer day, in about 1950, my friend and I were walking on this trail and we heard what sounded like someone operating an old rusty water pump. It was definitely coming from the marsh. We took off our shoes and started walking into the marsh toward the pump sound.

Low and behold, it got louder and there it was!! It was a bittern, or shy poke, sitting on a nest of eggs. Her beak was straight up in the air and she continued 'pumping'. She was nicely camouflaged and we got to within thirty feet of her.

This little stream flowed under the railroad tracks and eventually into Beaver Brook. The railroad trestle over the little stream was a fascination to us. It was about twenty-five feet above the water and scary to walk across.

After the stream went under the railroad tracks, it dropped fairly rapidly. In many places, it disappeared under the roots
~~~~~

of the trees. It might be out of sight for fifteen to thirty feet. It was a beautiful spot then and it is still beautiful today.

One December day, a week after deer season ended, my friend and I were walking along this stream. We saw some fish in some of the pools, so we shot at them with our .22 rifles. We were amazed to find out that we did not have to hit them, but the concussion of the bullet would stun them. The fish were brook trout. Boy, they were beautiful! We learned later that they were spawning and had come up from Beaver Brook during this time of the year to spawn.

My friend and I were beginning hunters and no one in either family had done much hunting of any kind. We were in his pasture one October afternoon and we saw a squirrel run up a tree. My friend had a .22 bolt action rifle, but I did not have a gun that day.

The squirrel ran up to the top of the tree and it was a windy day. We started taking shots at this squirrel, and after about 20 shots, we had apparently not hit it. However, we noticed the squirrel hanging upside down, and a few minutes later it was hanging by just two feet and, finally down it came. It was a red squirrel and one of our shots had creased its skull and didn't even make it bleed.

We took this little critter home, skinned it using a razor blade, gutted it out and cut it up. Then my friend's mother fried it for us. It was absolutely delicious!! We each had about three bites, but we were hooked. The next day we got a gray squirrel, which was much larger than the puny red squirrel we shot first.

This pasture was a wonderful place to explore for two young boys looking to broaden their horizons.

HOT STOVE

~~~~~

I started school at the Beaver Brook School in September of 1944, as a first grader. Miss N., from Sarona, was the teacher for about fifteen students in grades one through eight. My only first grade classmate was Dorothy and she was an Indian. We were good friends.

This school was closed forever in the spring of 1948 at the end of my fourth grade year. I really enjoyed school and the few classmates that I had. By the time the school closed, I had read every book in the small library. There was no television in those days, so I read a lot of books.

At recess, we sometimes played 'Annie-Annie I Over'. We would choose sides and someone threw a tennis ball over the one room school. The object was to tag all the players on the other side. There was a lot of running, yelling and laughing. We called 'pig tail' if the ball didn't get over the roof.

In later years, the boys would play football. One day I fell down in front of Jim, an older student, and he fell and broke his arm. My football career got started. In spring and fall, we played a lot of softball, or kitten ball, and all of the students played. Once a year, we went to the fairgrounds at Spooner and competed with other rural schools in a tournament. We also had a county wide track meet at the fairgrounds that was held in the fall of the year.

One winter, we got the idea of building an igloo. We gathered up most of the snow in the school yard and put it into a huge
~~~~~

pile. We hollowed it out for the igloo and then made another smaller igloo nearby. We connected both igloo's with a tunnel. Boy, was that ever neat! After several days, we climbed up on top and crashed through it.

We had Christmas programs, Mother's Day programs and various other programs that brought our parents and neighbors to the school. The school was the main focal point of our neighborhood.

We also held box socials and fun nights. For the box social, ladies and girls would pack a nice meal in a small box, such as a shoe box, and beautifully decorate it. No one knew which box belonged to which lady. These boxes would be auctioned off and the successful bidder ate the meal with the lady, or girl, who brought the box. It was a lot of fun. We then had a fishpond and other games that were played. I can still smell the coffee that was boiled in a huge pot on the stove. A raw egg, along with the broken egg shell, was put in the coffee pot to help settle the grounds.

Most of the kids either walked or rode bikes to school. The kids wore a variety of clothes, and bibbed overalls were common for both boys and girls. In those days, egg mash was fed to hens to help with egg production. This mash came in bags of colorful gingham prints that many mothers made into blouses, dresses, underwear, etc. We were not an impressive looking group, but we learned and had a lot of fun.

There was a County Superintendent of Schools who visited our school from time to time. One thing I remember about her is that she gave us some sort of standardized test to judge our IQ, etc. Otherwise, we had very few visitors.

We did listen to records. Peter & The Wolf was one. On one grand occasion, we were taken to Sarona to watch several movies with the Sarona students - two to three students sat together in each seat. WOW, that was exciting.

We did several things at night, some with the teacher, and some just the kids getting together. One cold October night, we were told there would be thousands of shooting stars. The night was clear and we all met up by Oscar's Store to watch. There were literally hundreds of shooting stars at all times.

Another time we went with the teacher down by the railroad tracks, under some large pine trees, and had a wiener roast and told scary stories. Another time was an all school fishing trip to Brown's Lake. One time we walked down to the artesian well and out to one of the dams on Beaver Brook.

About the time school started in 1944, we took mesh bags and went into the pastures and picked milkweed pods. We were told they would be used in Air Corps flier jackets. We also were encouraged to save our money to buy war bonds at school. We would take our dimes to school and the teacher would have stamps, one for each dime, that went into a small booklet. When the booklet was filled, we had enough to get a war bond.

Each class would have lessons with the teacher in the front of the room. We would sit on chairs in a semi-circle and the teacher would give us an assignment, then we went back to our seats to work. The older girls really enjoyed helping the little kids. In fact, that was probably the strongest feature of the country school - the older students helping the younger ones.

One cold January day, when I was in second grade, right after lunch, I had arithmetic with my teacher, Mrs. C. For whatever reason, I could not answer the question she had asked me and, she sent me to sit behind the stove. This was a big wood stove with a steel jacket around it and that day the stove was really hot!!

I sat in the corner trying to figure out the answer she wanted, but to no avail. She came over after each group and asked me if I knew the answer - for awhile. And then she forgot about me. Boy, it was hot in that corner!! Finally, recess came and the rest of the students went outside. I started to cry. I finally came out from behind the stove and started to walk toward the teacher. She saw me and shouted - OH, MY, I FORGOT ALL ABOUT YOU. She ran to me and apologized. She probably thought I was well done, as my face probably matched my red hair.

Anyway, she showed me the answer to the problem I was supposed to solve, it was worked out right there on the tear stained page in my book. Oh, well.

The last day of school was always a neighborhood picnic and everybody came, whether they had kids in school or not. After lunch, a big softball game was played, then school was over for the summer and vacation started. This meant we probably went barefooted after this day.

I look back on those years with happiness. I really enjoyed all that went on at school and was sorry it closed, but we got down to about ten students, so some of us went to Shell Lake and some went to Spooner. Today the old Beaver Brook school building stands as part of the Washburn County Museum complex in Shell Lake.

KOOL-AID STAND

~~~~~

The classic lemonade stand is an enterprise kids have done for many years. And kids will have lemonade stands for years to come. We had a Kool-Aid stand instead.

After World War II, people could sign up to buy a refrigerator. A far cry from today where you have many choices of refrigerators and other appliances. It was not that way in the late 1940s.

Finally, word was received that our refrigerator was in at a store in Shell Lake. I think Mom and Dad waited about two years for their name to come up. Actually, I believe it was in at the railroad depot and we could pick it up there. Local rail service was not the greatest in the 1940s. Dad said, "It probably went through Shell Lake a few times before it finally got switched out and unloaded here." I don't know if that was true or not. Anyway, it was ready to be picked up.

Dad hooked the trailer up to the back of the car and into town we went. The refrigerator was in a box made out of wood framing and a sort of wood veneer. We loaded it up and headed home. The refrigerator was uncrated and taken into the house and plugged in.

This was something new to our family who had lived with an icebox for many, many years. It had a small freezing compartment. We could keep ice cream in there. Besides, now we could make ice cubes.
~~~~~

The crate that the refrigerator came in fascinated us boys. Laying in on its side, it made a counter about the right height for kids. The light came on in our minds! How about a Kool-Aid stand. Yeah, let's do it! Mom? Mom and Dad reluctantly agreed to our plan.

We knew how to make Kool-Aid as that was about the only sweet drink we ever had. We seldom ever had pop. We pooled our finances and, went up to Oscar's Store and bought Kool-Aid and sugar. Sugar seemed to be fairly cheap at the time.

We got containers to carry water with ice cubes in, a container to mix the Kool-Aid in, a pitcher to serve it from and some glasses.

Next, we drew a sign on one side of the shipping crate 'ICE COLD KOOL-AID' - 5 cents. It wasn't pretty, but it told what our product was and what our price was.

Now, we had to get that crate and our product up to U. S. Highway 53, about an eighth of a mile uphill from our house. We thought about the wagon, but it was broken. We couldn't find the wheel barrow. Oh well, we can carry it. Oh, sure! That darn thing was heavy, at least for the three of us little boys. We grunted, groaned and sweated, but finally our Kool-Aid stand arrived on the shoulder of U. S. Highway 53, by the south bound lane.

We got ready to mix up a batch of Kool-Aid. What flavor? Finally, we decided on a flavor. In a pinch we could make up a special request.

I don't think we had high expectations and that was good because . . . . business was very slow. We spent the afternoon waving at people and, believe it or not, several did stop. Several people bought two cups.

When we finally called it quits, we had sold $1.30 worth of Kool-Aid. We figured our expenses were about $.40 so we had $.90 to split three ways. But, we still had sugar and Kool-Aid so we could sell again tomorrow, right? Wrong. We could drink it ourselves and that would solve that problem and that is exactly what we did.

The crate got hauled back home. The three of us learned a little about working together on our own project.

One of our customers was my 4th grade teacher, Mrs. T. She also had my two brothers in school, even though my youngest brother was not in school yet. He visited on many days, so this was a little like preschool, as it gave him a little head start for school.

FLUFFY

~~~~~

Fluffy was a long haired calico type mother cat that we had around our place in the mid-1940s. In those days, the basement in our house had a dirt floor. There was a window to the basement that had been left open and Fluffy got into the basement and had a litter of thirteen kittens. My parents decided to leave the window open so Fluffy could come and go as she needed.

One night, about two weeks later, a tomcat came into the basement and killed eleven of the thirteen kittens. Two kittens had crawled under the water heater so apparently the tom cat could not reach them. I know this is not an uncommon event in nature. Besides cats, boar bears will kill baby cubs. It must be to eliminate competition, and may also cause the mother to come into heat, and these males are more than willing to oblige.

Fluffy had other litters of kittens. One morning she came home dragging a full grown cottontail rabbit and fed it to her kittens. The rabbit was at least as large as Fluffy. This very nice, friendly cat was not a barn cat as were most of the cats on a dairy farm.

We always had cats in the barn, up to fifteen or so. In the winter they slept under the cows while the cows were standing up. Some slept on the cows back when the cow was lying down. It must have warmer there. From time to time, we found a flattened cat that had been laid on by a cow. Apparently, all cats are not 'as quick as a cat'. In those days, cats were not vaccinated for distemper and every few years most would die from the disease.
~~~~~

Most cats quickly learned to be near you when you began the process of milking a cow. Milking began by washing each teat and squirting some milk out of each teat. We would try to aim some milk at the waiting cats mouth and they would open their mouth to catch the milk. All the milk did not go into their mouths, so they would then spend a few minutes licking the milk off their fur.

One morning, my Dad could see something shiny on a fence post about 150 yards away. He told my brothers and me about it and we went to check it out.

It was a cat that had stuck its head into a can and got it stuck. The cat had somehow found the fence post and climbed up on it. We told Dad about it and he said to take some feed sacks, cover the cat and hold on. Then we should be able to pull off the can. We did this and the grateful cat ran off. It was not one of our cats.

Outside cats sometimes have the bad habit of climbing up under the hood of a warm car. Many cats are killed, or injured, by doing that. Many end up getting a ride to a new home. At least one cat was returned to us after riding to Spooner. Another cat rode to our place from Minong. The first day she was there, she crawled up on the wood furnace outside and promptly burned her tail, eventually most of it fell off.

This cat was very friendly and was a great jumper. If anyone came near her perch on lumber piles, etc., she would jump on your shoulder, back, head or whatever was handy. She would be purring like crazy, and you would have a hard time getting rid of her.

When our kids were small, they caught a very small kitten at their Grandma and Grandpa's farm. Smokey became a house cat and we found out he was a male as he began 'spraying' in the house to mark his territory. Boy, did that stink! But getting him neutered cured that. He was a great friend and lived for thirteen years. It was a sad trip to the veterinarian to put him down.

LADDIE

~~~~~

In about 1947, we acquired a yellow puppy. He was like most dogs around. This meant he was of mixed breeds. Some people had Border Collies or other dogs that they hoped would round up the cows and bring them in for milking.

We had no great expectations for Laddie. He grew to be a good sized dog of about 60-70 pounds. We had no clue about how to train a dog so between all parties we did a good job of turning out an untrained, hungry, but somewhat friendly dog.

He did not like to be bothered when he was eating something. Being somewhat adventurous, we would sometimes pester him when he was eating. We were paid in kind by getting bitten. We must have enjoyed the thrill of being able to get away without getting bit.

When Laddie was a half-grown puppy, I decided to buy him some wieners for Christmas. I took them home and told Laddie it was Christmas and this was his gift. I tossed one wiener to him and gulp! It was gone and he was looking for more. About three more gulps and I concluded that Laddie really didn't appreciate Christmas or my gift to him.

Laddie was like most of the other dogs that our neighbors had. They were fairly large and scary for a small kid. One dog in particular was one of the neighbor's dogs. I had to walk by it everyday on the way to school. The dog would
~~~~~

come out near me and bark like crazy. All the kids got the same treatment. He never bit anyone that I know of, but he was scary.

One day, my Mother had a meeting at this home and I was supposed to meet her there after school. This home had a short, open, wooden step with about four risers on it. Wouldn't you know it, this dog was lying under the steps and he was growling. I was in first grade and I was scared! I said, "Nice doggie." I took one more step. "Nice doggie." Then one more step. By now the tears started. I said, "Nice doggie", on each step up the stairs. Finally, I grabbed the door and ran into the house. This whole event lasted several minutes and I was super scared.

Most of the dogs around our neighborhood were untrained and would bark if someone came to the property. Many of these dogs had the habit of chasing cars. Some dogs would bite at the moving tires, others just ran along and barked at the car. Many dogs were killed in this manner, including Laddie.

Before Laddie died though, he was good at digging after gophers and catching snakes and shaking them. One day we were out in the woods and we saw a porcupine. Laddie saw it too, and stayed a little distance from it until it started up the tree. When the porcupine was about three feet up the tree, Laddie could not hold back any longer. He jumped up and bit the porcupine on the back! Poor Laddie, his face was loaded with quills. We went home, put a heavy blanket on him and all three of us kids piled on, and my Dad pulled out every quill. Laddie just laid there without a fuss.

One morning, two young guys pushed a disabled motorcycle into our yard. They asked if they could leave it there for a few days. Of course, Dad said, "yes." They also wanted to use the phone to get someone to pick them up.

Dad had just finished milking the cows and was washing the milking machines. Laddie was nearby and one guy asked Dad if the dog bites. Dad said, "No". You can guess what happened next. The guy reached out to pet Laddie and grrrrrrrr, Laddie had him by the wrist. That's about the way things go.

Later, at our place we had Barney and Fred. Barney was a hound of some kind and could really follow me if I left him home when I went hunting. Barney would be let out one hour or more after I left home to hunt. Several times Barney came running right on my trail. He was happy to see me, but I had to take him home and leave him locked up. I hated to do that and on occasion I drove to where I wanted to hunt and this apparently was more than Barney could handle.

Fred was half St. Bernard and weighed 125 pounds. Both dogs were very friendly and wanted to be with you all the time. Our family was partridge hunting on our farm one day with both Barney and Fred along. Betty said, "Fred has something here. Fred has a partridge!" Sure enough Fred had caught a partridge. It was not sick or hurt. Fred just went over and picked it up. He did that on another occasion, also.

Fred had fine hair and it was fairly long. One spring day we got 8-10 inches of wet, packy snow. Our family took a walk in the pasture and, of course Barney and Fred came along. The snow stuck to Fred's fur and collected in large snowballs. Eventually Fred could not walk because of the weight of the snowballs. We de-snowed him and continued for a distance before we had to stop and unload Fred again.

Our son had a beautiful black lab puppy named Velvet. She was a very friendly tail wagging dog. She liked chasing killdeer birds in our front pasture. She would spend hours of futility. One day she did catch a half-grown killdeer and brought it home to show us. That apparently satisfied her desire to chase killdeer.

Velvet went through a teething stage when she chewed on anything convenient. This included the lower end of the batten strips on our house. Velvets handiwork is visible today. One day our water pump did not work and I called the man who had installed our well. As I was talking to him on the phone I looked out of the window toward the pump. Low and behold, I could see that Velvet had chewed through the wire. Problem identified. I replaced the wire and the pump worked just fine. Lucky for Velvet that the pump wasn't running when she chewed.

The dogs were a joy to have around. Barney and Fred both had run-ins with porcupines - twice. It was a sad day when each of the dogs lives ended.

AMAZING DARE-DEVIL HELLDRIVERS

~~~~~

During the mid 1940s, my parents took my two younger brothers and me to the county fair at Rice Lake, Wisconsin. The grandstand show featured the HELLDRIVERS. These men and women drove cars over big jumps, jumped over moving cars and rolled their cars over.

To young boys in the pre-television era, this was really exciting! For the finale, they did several drives through fires and jumped over the fire.

On the way home to rural Shell Lake, my brothers and I talked about what we had seen. Boy, we were impressed by what these Helldrivers had done.

In the next day or two, we pretended we were Helldrivers. Of course, we did not have cars, not even bicycles, but we did have a wheel barrow. It was steel wheeled and full of cement remnants from hundreds of loads of concrete. But that did not seem to make a difference to us.

We got a plank and some wood and made a ramp. Each boy took turns riding in the wheel barrow. One boy took each of the handlebars and up the ramp the wheel barrow went. For a short while the rider was air borne, then came the crash. We quickly learned to not hang on to the wheel barrow when it landed because when it crashed, your fingers got pinched. Wow, this was very exciting! We tried riding backwards, standing up, laying down and on our knees to see which ride was the most exciting.
~~~~~

Eventually, I said, “Let’s jump through fire.” We gathered up wood scraps and built the pile of wood for the fire at the end of the ramp.

Next, we needed to get matches to get the fire going. We went to the house and found some matches. We had a gasoline barrel about a hundred feet from our proposed fire.

I was about eight or nine years old so I knew that gasoline makes things burn real good. I took a stick over to the gasoline barrel and ran some gas on it, as it lay on the ground under the gas faucet. Next, I lit a match and then the stick, as well as the other gasoline that ran out. There was a nice fire going - **right under the gas barrel!**

I ran to tell my older brother, who was about eighteen at the time. He came out and put the fire out and threatened to warm my bottom, but he could see his three little brothers had learned their lesson.

My parents were gone that afternoon and, when the story was relayed to them, my brothers and I were grounded. Our rough and tumble HELLDRIVER story came to an abrupt end.

HEDY AND FRED

~~~~~~

Hedy and Fred were friends of Mom and Dad. They had a farm about two miles south of our place on U. S. Highway 53, what is now known as Highway 253. When I was about nine or ten years old, Fred drove in to our place one summer day and asked my Dad if he could get one of the boys to help with haying and other work. The three of us were standing there and Dad said, "Take your pick." I felt like I knew what slaves were treated like. Now, don't get me wrong, Fred was a nice enough man, but I did not know him that well. No mention of pay was brought up, so I just figured I would not get paid. Oh, well, times were tough and he needed the help.

The first job Fred gave me was to take a full sized scythe and whack down thistles in the pasture. Several points of interest: this was a LOUSY job and there seemed to be thistles everywhere I looked. Then, he had Holstein cows and compared to our jerseys, these cows were huge and they seemed overly friendly and a few times I headed for the fence, but they really did not threaten me. It took me a long time to get used to them.

The other thing was that Fred always took a break in the middle of the morning and again in the middle of the afternoon, plus his noon lunch break. Hedy was quite an intellect and besides she put on a lot of great food. I think most of my thistle cutting days were spent looking forward to those breaks.
~~~~~~

Thankfully, Fred got around to putting up the hay. My only job was to drive tractor to make the loads and to pull up hay fork loads into the barn.

Fred was a very frugal farmer, as were most of them who had just survived the Great Depression and World War II. Fred made **giant** loads of hay using the hay loader. I drove the tractor, which was a nearly new Super C International. This was not a very big tractor and it would really labor going up a small hill.

One day, we were nearly done making a load and a small hill was ahead. I gave the tractor more gas thinking it would stall otherwise. Fred hollered down, "What are you trying to do - kill me?" I slowed down, and we did make it up the hill. You see, the faster you went, the faster hay came up the hay loader.

Finally, a giant load would be made and I would unhook the hay loader. Fred was trapped on top of the huge hay pile and he trusted me to get him, and the load of hay, safely to the barn. Remember, I was only nine or ten years old! He directed me from high up as I drove out onto Highway 53 and down to the barn. That part was really scary, especially if we met a semi-truck. I would pull up under the haymow door and now Fred could get off the load by climbing into the barn. I would unhook the tractor and hook it up to the hay rope and we unloaded the hay into the haymow.

I helped with other things that summer, too, and finally I was done and Fred paid me $10.00. WOW! I was convinced that I had been working for free. Now I had to take back some of those thoughts that had gone through my head.

About a year later, one winter Sunday, our family was invited to dinner with Fred and Hedy. Mr. & Mrs. R. were also invited. We began eating dinner, which included a lettuce salad. I took a bite of the salad and bit into a piece of soap. I announced for all to hear, "There is soap in this salad." Hedy and my Mom were horrified. Mom wanted me to hush up, and I said, "I guess I know what soap tastes like." Poor Hedy was fit to be tied as she examined the part of a bar of soap still on my plate. Mrs. R. finally figured out what had happened. The big bowl of salad was placed in the sink for mixing. Someone picked up the wash cloth, which was on the bar of soap, and as it passed over the salad the soap fell in and then got mixed in. The salad was examined and there it was, the rest of the bar of soap. Part of the bar had broken off and that is what I had munched on.

I worked for Fred on and off through high school. I helped saw logs into lumber, and I helped build his new barn in about 1954. Fred got attacked by his bull and spent a few weeks in the hospital. His neighbor, the father of one of my friends, had been killed by a young bull just prior to this time.

Fred had a double barreled 12 gauge shotgun. It was a Fox Model B and was hammerless. When I was about thirteen, he let me borrow it one winter so I could use it to fox hunt. The snow was so deep that I hunted on skis. I went by a brush pile on my right and out ran a fox. I am right-handed and I didn't get my skis apart and accidentally pulled both triggers on the double barrel. I went right over on my back. I hit the fox, but didn't hurt it because the thick fur trapped the pellets.

Hedy was probably my Mom's best friend. They both were very intelligent and widely read. They got into many deep discussions about the issues of the day and politics in general. When my Mom passed away, Hedy wrote a poem honoring Mom and had it printed in the Shell Lake newspaper. It was very touching.

BIG BROTHER

~~~~~

My oldest brother was nine years older than me. Needless to say, he was much larger than me in the late 1940s. My younger brothers and I would gang up on him during wrestling matches, probably with one brother hanging on his head. We were not much of a threat to him, but maybe next year! He also was on the boxing team at Shell Lake Schools so he taught us how to box. I did not care much for getting my face punched.

We used to live in Gilmanton, Wisconsin and in 1939 we moved to Shell Lake. My brother's friend from Gilmanton spent most of the summers at our place during their high school years and then he moved to Oregon. He had asthma and gave himself a daily shot in the leg.

About the time I was eight or nine, my brother bet me that I could not get 50 sticks of bubble gum in my mouth at one time. I had a big mouth so I said I could. He bought the bubble gum, actually bubble gum balls for a penny apiece, but he ended up with fifty-six bubble gum balls. I started in by chewing five or six at a time to get rid of the candy shell. Eventually, I got all fifty-six sticks in my mouth at once so, I did not have to pay for them. This is a picture of me in my bibbed overalls, barefooted, with my mouth full of the 'cud' of bubble gum. The trees in the background are about four feet tall and today they are over 50 feet tall.

One summer about that time, Dad wanted my brother to
~~~~~

clear some land by cutting the small trees down. One day he took me along to help. We had a can of Spam that we cooked over a fire at noon. While sitting around after eating, he made a deal with me. He said, "If you eat two ants you will not have to help this afternoon." I debated about this deal and finally agreed to do it. We found two little red ants and I ate them! Boy, they tasted terrible. When I got done eating them, he held up his hand and showed that his fingers were crossed so he said our deal was off. I was mad at him, but he thought it was funny.

Another time, a year or two later, I had picked some cones from a Tamarack tree and was showing them to Dad and my brother while they were milking the cows. These cones are small, about the size of the end of your little finger. My brother says, "How much will you give me if I eat two cones?" I thought there is no way he would do that so I said, "Fifty cents," which was about my total net worth then. That pot-likker took those two cones, popped them in his mouth, chewed them up and swallowed them. I had to pay up and, later I remembered that I should have had my fingers crossed behind my back, but I didn't. Oh, well. I think that was about the last time he hood-winked me, though.

Dad had an old F-14 Farmall tractor that had to be cranked by hand to get it started. It was difficult to get started if there was any humidity in the air. The distributor cap had to be wiped dry and then, with any luck, it might start. My brother and his friend spent a lot of energy getting that tractor running.

My big brother went into the air force for twenty-nine years. He rose to the rank of Lieutenant Colonel and was a pilot on C-124 airplanes.

THE BULL IN THE SILO PIT

~~~~~~

In the late 1940s, on my parents' farm near Shell Lake, we had a nice herd of jersey cows. We also had a jersey bull. He had a long chain attached to a strong leather halter and also to the ring in his nose.

The bull was tethered on this long chain so as cows came up for water he could detect them in heat and do his 'bully' duties. His chain was attached to the southwest corner of the barn. There was a hole cut in the barn where we could feed the bull.

The barn was new in 1942, but the silo was a reconstructed wooden stave affair. Typical of silos in those days, it had a pit that extended eight feet, or more, into the ground. About this time, a strong wind blew the empty silo down leaving the exposed empty pit.

For whatever reason, the bull fell into the pit and his chain was long enough for him to be able to reach the bottom of the pit without getting hung up.

I was about ten years old and can remember the bull in the pit looking up at us, pawing the ground, apparently unhurt. We lowered water and feed down to him and my Dad contemplated how we would get him out of the pit.

My dad, Walter Hubin, was an ingenious inventor and this would be like going for the state championship if he could get the bull out without hurting him.

After a few days, he devised a plan. It required the use of the
~~~~~~

wrecker from the Ford dealer in Shell Lake. Dad rigged up two large poles attached at the top with a large pulley hanging below the top. These two poles were leaned over the silo so the pulley was over the center of the pit.

For the life of me, I can not remember how my Dad got the harness under the bull. He made a contraption that put two large straps under the bull, one behind the front legs and one in front of the back legs. Heavy rope went up through the pulley and was attached to the winch of the wrecker.

Dad was a wizard with numbers and he calculated how far the rope would have to be raised to bring the bull above the edge of the silo. Once that was calculated, he tied a big knot in the rope in precisely the right spot. The theory was that as the bull was pulled up the knot would hit the pulley and slowly tip the two poles toward the wrecker and transport the bull gently out of the pit and onto the ground.

The moment of truth arrived and the winch was started. Low and behold, up came the bull. However, the bull was kicking and squirming, not being used to this kind of levitation. Magically, the knot reached the pulley and the two poles swung toward the wrecker and the bull landed on the ground outside of the pit. However, with all of his kicking he got the chain wrapped around his feet. When he landed, the ring pulled out of his nose. That must have hurt really bad.

The chain was still attached to his halter so the dazed and bewildered bull could be controlled. I don't remember if the bull was really upset, but generally those jersey bulls were very dangerous.

Eventually, my Dad got a chance to reflect on his engineering marvel. The bull's chain was shortened and the silo reconstructed. Apparently, filling the silo pit with hay or sawdust and letting the bull walk out was not an option for Dad.

Dad kept that bull around for several more years and he produced many high quality jersey calves. His nose, however, was torn on the bottom so when he smelled a cow his nose extended like an elephant's trunk. *That was a sight to see*!

HAYMOW BASKETBALL

~~~~~

From seventh grade on through high school, basketball was of great interest to me and my friends. Nearly everyone had a basketball and a hoop and, if we had some time to spare, we would shoot baskets or play ball.

Winter weather and snow presented a problem, but if we fed the hay out of the east end of the haymow, we could put the basket on the end inside of the haymow. We would hang up two or three lights and we were good to go. Never mind the longies and winter clothes we wore. We really liked shooting baskets and playing ball.

With a little planning, we could get enough kids to make teams which we did one or two evenings each week, mainly in February and March. We would choose sides and everyone played, regardless of size or skill. The game went on for a couple of hours and for the most part they were friendly games, but competition was keen at times.

Now, the haymow floor was made of shiplap and we would break through in places. When we fell through, we probably got a scratched leg and time was called while we found a board to nail over the hole in the floor. Eventually the floor had a dozen or more board patches. It made it hard to dribble the ball, but we didn't care. Most of us were lousy dribblers anyway, and besides it forced us to pass more. However, most of us could shoot pretty good. We also could rebound with authority. Our defense was very basic, just 'clobber 'em'. Needless to say, we had a lot of fun and used up a great deal of energy.
~~~~~

The *Minneapolis Lakers* were winning world championships in the 1950s. We would see them on snowy television, or the movie shorts, from time to time. We tried to emulate George Mikans' hook shot, even though we were about a foot shorter than he was. Vern Mikkelson had a great jump shot which, believe it or not, nobody around Shell Lake did before then. We used one or two handed set shots.

When not competing, we worked on shooting, following shots and rebounding. Kids of that time were excellent shooters. There was no 3- point line then and many of my shots in high school would have been 3 pointers. Guess I was born 30 years to soon.

The Globe Trotters came to Rice Lake twice and Dad took several of us to watch. Wow, some of these players were tall - I mean 6'10" or so. Those guys were great, making long shots, drop kicks and other gags. They could really handle the ball, dribble and pass.

Back to the haymow. We could play in the haymow until we put hay up some time in July. However, darkness didn't arrive until late and besides summer meant other activities, but we still organized games especially on rainy days or nights.

When it was time to put hay in, the basket was taken down, and not put up again until the haying was done. The reason for that was where we put the basket up outside was where we pulled the hay up into the barn.

Later on, we played Sunday afternoon in the Sarona Town Hall. Just make up games, but a lot of fun. In the summer, we played at the beach at Shell Lake, which had a cement basketball court and this attracted kids from all over. We saw some pretty good players and enjoyed playing with and against them. During this time, Shell Lake had some good basketball teams and this court at the beach certainly played a role in it.

When we could play basketball in the gym at school, it was a real treat. No heavy clothes, nice floor and you could bounce the ball without it bouncing off a patch on the floor. I was good about bouncing it off my foot, or knee, after about two bounces. I did play all four years in high school and I really enjoyed it.

HALLOWEEN

~~~~~

Stories of Halloween pranks when my Dad was young were far different than what was happening in my day. He told of taking buggies apart, taking them to the top of a barn and putting them back together. Another time a group of boys stacked firewood in front of all the doors of a neighbor's house. Other pranks were equally laborious, but were not malicious.

I do remember someone took our dump rake and pulled it up to the peak of the barn using the big hay rope. One time someone let a few chickens loose in the Shell Lake High School office. There was also a cow let loose in the school on another occasion. None of my friends did things like that, as far as I know.

There always were stories of outhouses being pushed over. There were a few outhouses still around in the 1950s, in fact one of our neighbors had one.

My friend and I got the idea that we should roam around the neighborhood on a beautiful clear moonlight night on Halloween in about 1951. It was spooky because we wondered if there were other people doing the same thing. It was about as bright as day while we went through pastures and fields and came near people's buildings. We did not have any plan, but we were enjoying being 'sneaky'.

Eventually, we came near the home of the neighbor with an outhouse. We sneaked up close, and then watched and waited. Of course, we could picture this person sitting in
~~~~~

the shadows with a shotgun. We also wanted to be sure no one was in the building as we certainly did not want to hurt anyone.

After a long, nervous wait while straining to see if we could see anyone in the shadows, we decided to move up to the building. Boy, we were scared!! We had heard of people moving their outhouses a few feet forward, so when the pranksters went to push, they fell in the pit - YUCK!

We carefully inspected to be sure that hadn't happened with this outhouse. We double checked for anyone with a shotgun and then pushed . . . . and pushed . . . . and pushed. That building must have been bolted to a foundation. Boy, we were relieved! I guess we really didn't want to damage anything anyway.

We back tracked out of there, expecting a shotgun blast at any second. We continued exploring in the moonlight, feeling good that we had attempted a prank, but feeling better that we had not done it. It was hard to figure, but we were half grown boys who were trying to figure things out.

The first thing I can ever remember of Halloween happened one Halloween night when I was helping my mother do dishes. I was not in school yet and did not know anything at all about Halloween. Taking kids trick or treating did not happen in our neighborhood in the mid 1940s.

I was drying a dish when all of a sudden this bright orange face appeared at a dining room window. It scared me so much I dropped the dish and hid behind my mother's legs. I probably cried.

It was the neighbor kids and that bright orange face was a jack-o-lantern. Mom invited them in so I could see their jack-o-lantern. I knew these kids and was much relieved once I could see it was a pumpkin.

FIRST DEER HUNT

~~~~~~

I would finally be able to hunt deer in the fall of 1951. I bought a license and would hunt with my friend, along with his Mom and Dad. My friend's Dad delivered fuel and had been invited to hunt up by Springbrook with Jim. My Dad knew Jim because he was a World War II Veteran and my Dad taught a farm program that Jim was enrolled in. He could receive the GI bill funds for doing this.

The night before the season started, I stayed at my friend's home. I had all my gear with me, including the army rifle. Both of us were really excited. We both collected ammunition and he had an Italian cartridge that was about like my .30-06. We put it in the gun and it got stuck! We spent an hour, or more, before we got that darn shell out of my gun. Neither of us slept that night. We were too excited.

We arrived at Jim's place at Oh, Dark Thirty, and Jim was still in bed. He hopped out, put a couple slices of bread on the top of the stove to toast and he was good to go. Jim was not above taking some government beef when the opportunity presented itself. He told of seeing a deer walk on the road outside of his house. He said he wanted that deer real bad, so he shot right through the window of his house.

We arrived at the woods and in we went. We spent the day making drives, standing and not seeing any deer.

In 1951, there were not many deer in northern Wisconsin.
~~~~~~

Deep snow had killed them by the thousands. We did see a couple fresh tracks and this was great looking hardwood ridges country.

Late in the afternoon, Jim put my friend on one side of a ravine, and I was on the other side. He went to drive that ravine to us. After a half hour or so, I heard my friend shoot. Boy, I was so excited. When we got together later, my friend said he had shot, but not at a deer. He had a Model 94 Winchester .30-30 and was cocking and uncocking the gun out of boredom. The hammer slipped out from under his thumb and it went off. That was scary!

It was getting late in the day and we headed for Jim's house. Jim's wife met us and told that the neighbor had wounded a deer and Jim was to keep his hands off from it. Jim said, "Let's go find it." It was a small deer and wounded in one of its hind quarters. We trailed it into a freshly cut woods and Jim said, "We will get it in the morning."

Next morning, bright and early, we went with Jim to get this deer. Jim and I would stand while my friend and his Dad would take the trail. It was very cold and still. Pretty soon I could hear something walking. It got louder and louder and then - BANG. Jim shot it.

I went over to Jim and there lay the deer. It was small, but a deer. My friend and his Dad came up, and his Dad said, "Boy, that is smaller that I thought it would be." Jim said, "Ya, they get a lot bigger than this one." We dressed it out, and Jim gave it to us. We drew straws to see who would get the shot up quarter of the deer. I was the lucky one!

I never did see a live deer that year. My friend's Dad shot a doe across the tracks in the Beaver Brook Wildlife area. He had a .30-40 Craig Bolt action rifle.

I have hunted deer about 60 years and have bagged many bucks, but that first hunt is very memorable to me. Probably the next most memorable was when I took my grandson, Dexter, with me down in the Beaver Brook Wildlife area in 2004. We went to the Beaver Pond and the site of the old sluice dam on Beaver Brook. Later that day, we walked to the trestle over the little stream that ran out of my friend's old pasture. We went downstream on this little stream to see if any trout were spawning yet and we did not see any.

We devised a plan to hunt our way back to the truck. I was close to the stream and Dexter would be close to the old railroad bed, as the tracks had been removed and was now an ATV snowmobile trail. We were going to sneak hunt. I had not gone more that 200 yards, when all of a sudden, I heard that awful sound - a big deer was running nearby - there it was!! A beautiful big buck had jumped out of its bed and was running flat out and only about 30 yards away, but between Dexter and me. I could not shoot, but what a beautiful sight. I did not even feel bad that I could not get a shot at that beautiful animal.

EXPLORERS

~~~~~

When I was in the seventh grade, my neighbor and friend, and I were really into exploring. We had tramped through all nearby woods and pastures. The big woods on the other side of the railroad tracks was off limits, but we were really tempted.

Finally, during teachers convention, in the first part of October, we decided to go just a little way beyond the tracks. We had a .22 rifle between us and we were fairly good woodsmen - after all we had been Cub Scouts!

We really did not know much about this big woods except that we thought it was big. Cautiously, we started into this forbidden woods. Really, it looked like most of the other woods around there, so we kept going.

Lo and behold, we came to a stream. We were excited. We must have discovered a secret stream, but, look! On the other side it looks like a path. Must have been made by Indians!! Boy, were we scared. Then we thought, the few Indians we knew were all nice folks, so we continued on, but were careful to mark our trail so we could find our way home.

We found a log to cross the stream on and now we were on the trail. Funny how it seemed to lead to certain spots in the stream and then continue on. Not being trout fishermen then, we did not realize this trail was made by trout fishermen and this was Beaver Brook, a very good trout stream.
~~~~~

Beginning the next summer, I fished Beaver Brook and have done so dozens of times over the next 50 years. I have great memories of my fishing trips on Beaver Brook.

By mid-afternoon, we were well down stream. A few feet from Beaver Brook, we found a beaver dam. It dammed up spring water and made about a five acre pond. The dam was about five feet high and very impressive.

We continued on and about 150 yards downstream, we came to four big timbers placed across the stream, which by now was much wider. What the heck were these four 12" x 12" timbers doing spanning this stream? We could walk across on these. Today, these four timbers are still there but underneath the water and much worn down.

Today, we also know this was part of a sluice dam used by the turn of the century loggers to hold water behind these dams in the spring during spring melt. Logs were piled along the banks downstream. This dam was strategically placed at the end of a natural valley and probably made about a five acre lake up to six feet deep. The dam would be opened and a big flood of water was released. The logger rolled the logs into the flood and with any luck the logs ended up at their sawmill.

By this time, the two explorers, meaning my friend and I, noted that the sun was very low and we had better hustle our buns for home, besides this was scary country. We made it back to the railroad tracks and back home, but it was almost dark. Boy, had we had an exciting day! We did have to fess up that we had crossed the tracks. I don't remember that anything bad happened to us for punishment.

Looking back at that beautiful October day, it was one of the most enjoyable of my life. It was full of mystery and intrigue. It gave two teenagers quite a thrill.

BOUNTY HUNTER

~~~~~

In the 1940s, critters were a threat so war was declared on certain species. Bounties were paid on foxes, crows and gophers. Hawks were a threat to chickens, so were owls, so war was declared on them, too, but no bounty was put on their heads.

The bounty on gophers was five cents per tail. We tried to shoot them with our single shot .22 rifle. We would wait near one of their burrows until they came out. For whatever reason, the gophers liked burrows at the base of a wooden fence post.

The striped gopher is not a big animal, but when it stood up on its hind legs it appeared to be about a foot high. It would make a whistling sound if it got scared. You could spend a lot of time waiting and maybe no gopher showed up at all.

We had a yellow, non-descript dog by the name of Laddie. If he suspected there was a gopher is a hole, he would begin digging. One day he was digging northwest of the barn and my brothers and I were watching. Boy, that dog could make the dirt fly.

After digging the hole about a foot deep, he stopped digging as he could not find the gopher. I knelt by the hole and probed the sides to find the hole that was filled in with dirt. My fingers found the hole and in it was the gopher. He proceeded to bite my finger. Of course, I howled and pulled my finger out and the gopher was still attached. I pulled so hard that the gopher went flying about 20 feet into the air. When it
~~~~~

came down, Laddie was on it and made short work of that gopher. I had a hole in my fingernail and a matching one below it, but we would be five cents richer.

Crows were a real challenge. I had purchased a 12 gauge single barrel shot gun when I was in seventh grade. It cost me $7.00, and it kicked like a mule. I tried sneaking up on crows in our pasture, but they are very wary. I swear that they spotted me about the time I left home and spread the word to 'look out'!

Bounty on crows was $.25 a head. Shot gun shells were $.12 each, so if I got a crow with every other shot I could at least break even. I didn't shoot many crows for a long time.

One June evening, near dark, I was out in the woods and I could hear a bunch of crows in a big oak tree. I sneaked under the tree and looked up and there were several crows, maybe getting ready to roost for the night. I picked out a crow and fired. Flames shot out, but down came a crow! I picked it up and went home. That night as I was lying in bed, I thought, "I think I saw another crow fall." I went back the next morning and sure enough there lay another crow. That was fifty cents with one shot.

There was big money in fox bounty. It was $5.00 for an adult and $2.50 for a young one. There was no season on foxes or crows like there is now. When I was in high school, my friends and I tried to find fox dens to dig out and get the little pups.

One early spring morning, it had just snowed and I picked

up a fox track and followed it to a den. I went and got my buddies and we came with shovels and started digging. We dug down about seven feet and finally found five little fox pups. They were cute, gray with blue eyes and a white tip on their tail.

We each took one home. My little fox cried all night long. It would drink milk from an eye dropper, but it would not stop crying. After a day or two of this crying, my Mom said, "No more." Dad took it to the courthouse to get the $2.50 for me. The lady there said, "I'll pay $2.50 for that cute little thing." I don't know what ever happened to that little fox. We tried digging out a couple other dens, but to no avail.

Eventually, there were no more bounties. As beautiful as fox fur was, there was no sale for the pelts. In the 1960s and 1970s, fox pelts were worth $20-$50 each. This prompted more trapping of fox and about this time more hunters used hounds to get the fox. Today, there are a lot less foxes around. That is too bad.

THE ARTESIAN WELL AND THE TUNNEL

~~~~~

I attended the Beaver Brook School from 1944 to 1948. There were never over 15 kids in all the grades 1-8. The school was located four and one-half miles east of Shell Lake, Wisconsin and one-half mile from an artesian well. This well was put in by the Badger Cranberry Company in the 1930s. It was so dry the cranberry company thought they would not have enough water to flood when there was frost in late summer. The water was to cover the berries to keep them from being hurt by the frost.

The well had an eight inch casing and, lo and behold, water flowed out all on its own. Later, my Dad wired a large electric motor to pump water faster than the well normally ran.

This well was located a few feet from the Beaver Brook stream, and upstream from the reservoir where water was stored for flooding. It was also just a few feet from County Road B and an electric line ran nearby to power the motor.

This well was a great attraction for kids, as we would kneel down and get a drink from this very cold stream of water. Today, the building that housed the motor is gone and a nice cap has been put on the casing. Water flows out so people can get a drink and fill containers. It is really cool. It also is now part of the Beaver Brook Wildlife Area and is owned by the State of Wisconsin. It is under the supervision of the Wisconsin Department of Natural Resources.
~~~~~

Just up the hill from the well was the railroad track that ran between Eau Claire and Superior. This line was built about 1878 and was one of the main modes of transportation that people used to get here to settle northwest Wisconsin.

About 150 yards north of Highway B is an amazing tunnel under the railroad tracks. It was made of small to large limestone blocks and is about eight feet wide, eight feet high and about sixty feet long with an arched ceiling. The largest stone must have weighed 500 pounds, or more, and I have marveled at the skill of the builders. I have also wondered how the tunnel was built. The tunnel carried rainwater under the railroad tracks.

This tunnel was within sight of the Beaver Brook School and about 200 yards from where my friend, Gary, lived. He was in my class during third and fourth grade. His family lived in what was at one time the 'section crew house'. In other words, the crew that took care of that section of the railroad lived there previous to Gary and his family.

After school and on weekends, the tunnel was a great attraction. It was our secret hiding place. Also, we were getting our courage up to stay in the tunnel when a train went over. It took me several tries to finally stay in the tunnel when a train crossed over.

This period of time was when the steam engines were being replaced by diesel power. Also, iron ore was being hauled on this line to the steel mills near Chicago. The track runs uphill from Spooner to Sarona so these ore trains had three diesel engines at the front and two pushing at the rear. The ore was very heavy and the trains really labored along at four to five miles per hour. An hour or so after the train went south, the two pushing engines went back to Spooner. Sitting in the tunnel when these engines came back was a good way to get broken in so you could stay when a big train came by. The tunnel and artesian well are both very much like they were when I was a kid. It brings back memories of days long gone by.

THE 1937 FORD

~~~~~

The first car I can remember my parents owning was the 1937 Ford. It was the only automobile type machine we had at our place. It was used for more that just hauling people.

My Dad was an electrician and had a large trailer that he pulled with the car. The '37 Ford had a spring bumper in front and back. This was a band of chrome steel that stuck out of the front and back of the car.

One day, Dad was backing up to hook on to the trailer when the tongue went up and the trailer rolled forward. The tongue put a huge scratch in the trunk door that looked really ugly, and it never got fixed.

This car had fenders above the front wheels, big enough to sit on. We fed ground feed to the cows, so Dad sometimes hauled this feed home on, and in, the car. He would have two 100 pound bags on the front bumper, and one over each fender. At least two bags were put in the trunk and with the lid put down, he put one bag on the top of the trunk. This car was a two door, but Dad would put several bags in the back seat, and at least one in the front seat. He possibly could have put two on the rear bumper, but I am not sure of that. He must have put extra air in the tires to haul that much weight. This was really a strange sight to see. It also was a source of amusement to the neighbors.

We did not get a refrigerator until about two years after the end of World War II. We kept food cool in an icebox that sat on the back porch. This was a wooden case with a lot of
~~~~~

insulation and several doors that opened to compartments. A big block of ice was put in the very top of the ice box and as the ice melted, the water ran out of a drain and off the porch. The cool air would settle downward keeping the food cool.

Depending on the temperature, a block of ice only lasted two to four days. When more ice was needed, Dad would stop at the ice house in Shell Lake just before he came home from town. Mr. J. operated the ice house and he would go into the shed where the ice was kept under sawdust, dig out a block, pick it up with a pair of ice tongs and put it on the front bumper of the '37 Ford. By the time Dad got home, there would be a deep groove melted into the ice from the bumper, plus the 60-70 pound block of ice lost a lot of water on a hot day. The ice would be boosted up into the ice box and we would be able to keep the food cool for a few days.

I do know that there were days when the icebox had no ice in it, so food wasn't as cool as it should be. Mom was good at getting food used before it spoiled. Chicken was a good summertime meat because our family could eat one or two of them before it needed refrigeration. The same with fish. Otherwise, people butchered hogs and beef in the fall to take advantage of winter refrigeration. Mom also canned chicken and it was delicious.

There were no new cars built during World War II as all factories were put to work making airplanes, trucks, tanks, ships, etc. Mom and Dad finally bought a new car in 1949, also a Ford. It was a radical design, no good for hauling feed sacks. There were no fenders or extruding bumpers on it. By this time we got the feed delivered to our farm.

One trip to town with the '37 Ford was memorable. As we went near the cemetery, the hood all of a sudden flew up and we could not see a thing. That put a nice dent in the hood. It kind of evened out the big scratch on the trunk.

Also, one day near the cemetery, we found a crate of muskmelon laying scattered about on the road. We picked the melons up and then we waited to see if anyone would return. No one came, so we took them home and proceeded to eat the melons to our heart's content, as they would not keep. Boy that was great.

Poor Mom!! She was just learning to drive and the old '37 Ford was a real challenge to her. It had a floor shift, and the clutch and gas balance remained mysterious until they got a 1955 Ford with an automatic transmission. Mom dreaded having to drive that '37 Ford and invariably she revved the engine more that was needed before backing up or going forward. Once she got the car shifted into third gear, she was OK, but that could be 'herky jerky'.

If the electricity went off, Dad would use the '37 Ford to run the milking machine. This worked because the windshield wipers worked on vacuum in those days, and so did milking machines. While driving, if you had the wipers going in the rain and tried to pass someone, your vacuum wipers stopped working as you stepped on the gas, so you could not see.

My first attempt to drive the '37 Ford came at about age seven. The car was parked up by the barn (probably to unload feed). My brother and I got in and pretended to drive, like all kids do. I shifted the car out of gear and the car began rolling backward, as there was a slight grade there. The car finally hit a chunk of cement about forty feet from where it started. This, however, crunched the exhaust pipe. Apparently the emergency brake was not set, or maybe it didn't work. I got a lesson on not fiddling with the shifting lever.

Dad let me drive out in the fields, and I did sneak out on the road before I had a license or even a learner's permit. Things were so much different in those days.

The old '37 Ford was abandoned and left behind the machine shed until well into the 1970s. Someone saw it and wanted to buy it, so it was sold. People like to fix up these old cars and the '37 Ford had lots of character. I wonder if it is still being used.

MOOSUCK AND THE BULL OF THE WOODS

~~~~~

Any child growing up on a farm had to help with the chores, whatever they were. My folks raised jersey cows and we all helped with chores, except Mom. All dairy herds in our neighborhood were small, not over 40 cows. The most we ever milked was 31 cows.

In the 1940s and 1950s the milk was shipped to the creamery in ten gallon cans that had the farmer's name and account number on each can. The biggest farmers shipped eight to ten cans per day.

Naming cows and calves was a family project. Each animal had to have just the right name because of its color, temperament, size or anything else that made it unique, like horns. 'Bell', 'Molly' and 'Betsy' were some that come to mind.

And then there was Moosuck! What a cool name. She was an ordinary cow, except for one thing. She was a fence runner. If there was a weak spot in the fence, Moosuck found it and got out. The next thing, someone driving by on the highway would stop and tell us there was a cow out. We would go and chase her back in and fix the fence.

This went on for some time. Moosuck was warned that if she did not change her ways, some changes would be made. I don't think she listened. The next step was to make a yoke and put it on her. This consisted of 1" x 6" boards, bolted
~~~~~

and nailed together and put around her neck. The idea was that the yoke would not go through the fence. And it worked! That was a real sight to see. Eventually Dad took it off and for whatever reason, she did not get out after that.

The Bull in the Woods was the other unique cow name. She was a large cow and must have been the boss cow. Cows are like most other animals and have a pecking order in the social structure of the herd or flock. From time to time, fights would break out among the cows as disputes were settled. New cows added to the herd would have to establish their position among the herd. But the Bull in the Woods remained the boss.

THE HEARSE

~~~~~

Approximately 1948, my Dad bought a power takeoff manure spreader. It was made by Skyline. It was one of the first power takeoff spreaders in our neck of the woods. This meant the power takeoff shaft on the tractor powered the spreader.

Most other spreaders were ground driven. As the wheels turned, this unloaded the manure. These spreaders were not very big and you had to load them in such a way that they did not plug up.

This power takeoff spreader of Dad's may have worked alright the first year or two, but then things started to go wrong. We had an 8N Ford tractor. We kept the tractor and the manure spreader in the barn in the winter time.

During my high school years, it was my job to clean the barn out by hand, once in the morning and once in the evening. This meant taking the load of manure out and spreading it. Some days or nights it was really a challenge. The cold, windy, snowy conditions, getting stuck, breakdowns, etc., made it a real challenge.

Anyway, the Skyline spreader got to the point that it would not ratchet or unload like it was supposed to all the time. When this happened, I had to take a pipe wrench and put it on the end of the shaft and help it along. Dad worked on solving this problem and eventually he did.

His solution was to get a direct current motor, mount it so it
~~~~~

could drive a belt that drove the shaft when it needed help. This meant there was a wire leading from the battery on the tractor to the motor on the spreader. Probably the first electric over power takeoff spreader in existence. There was a switch on the wire so when help was needed we just flipped the switch. It worked well.

Several years passed and all the bearings had to be replaced. Dad made them out of hard maple boiled in oil. We went through several apron chains which, of course, broke with a full load on. Lots of fun fixing that!!

Dad struggled with that spreader for many years. It was his personal challenge to make it work. One day he was making an adjustment on the chain drive to the top beater. In order to do this, the spreader had to be running. He doesn't know how, but somehow he got his thumb under the chain and between the sprocket. The tractor was idling so it took a while for his thumb to come out the other side of the sprocket - **OUCH!** Needless to say, it broke his thumb but luckily it didn't cut it off. Probably because the spreader was worn out.

Eventually, Dad admitted defeat and bought a different spreader. He spent countless hours repairing, rebuilding, adjusting and cussing at the Skyline spreader, which he maintained must have been the only one ever made. Surely the company would not be able to duplicate 'Rube Goldberg' and find some sucker gullible enough to buy it.

You may have wondered about the title of this story, The Hearse. Well, kids think of names, so the spreader was called 'THE TURD HEARSE'. There, now you know the rest of the story!

REYNARD

~~~~~~

On winter weekends, when I was in high school, I tried to hunt fox whenever I could. There was no season on them at that time and, in fact, Washburn County paid a $5.00 bounty for an adult fox brought to the court house. The hides had no value in those days. Today the pelts are quite valuable.

One of the most beautiful things I have ever seen is a full grown red fox in its winter fur all fluffed out with its black legs and black ears against the white snow. The fox is a very worthy adversary as they are clever and wary.

In the days of the early 1950s, we had deep snow so I went looking for Reynard on skis. Most winters, by January or February, the snow would be so deep and drifted that I could ski right over most fences.

The fox is most active at night so by day it will sleep. It looks for a south exposure so the sun light will be absorbed by the red fur. The fox will curl up on the snow. My strategy was to ski to these south exposed hillsides in search of Reynard while it was sleeping. I tried to get close enough to get a shot but most times it ran off. It would also go into its den to sleep in the winter.

One particular fox had lost part of its right hind leg below the knee. It was not noticeable unless the snow was deep and then you would see a small hole in the snow instead of a foot print.

This fox perplexed me for three winters. It would lay out in
~~~~~~

a depression in a large field, and whenever I approached, it would see me and run off before I could get a shot at it. I tried approaching from different directions. I had one of my brothers come from the east and I waited to the north but the fox did not show up.

For whatever reason, this fox had a sixth sense when it came to me. I never did get it. I spent a lot of time trailing the fox after it ran, hoping for a shot, but to no avail.

Once, I trailed a fox I had seen and it headed west. I was right behind it in the woods and all of a sudden a partridge erupted out of the snow and scared me big time. The fox had gone within two feet from where the partridge roosted under the snow and he had not smelled it. Snow is good insulation and apparently also good at blocking the scent.

About 1948, a red fox came within about 75 feet of our house, hopped over a snow fence, and caught two young chickens from a flock we had confined there. There also was a small house in the enclosure. This all happened about 9:00 or 10:00 o'clock in the morning. The fox bit off the wings and feet of both chickens, which were about half grown, hopped back over the snow fence with both birds, perhaps one at a time, and went across a freshly plowed field straight for her den.

Foxes are not nearly as big as they look. I've weighed every one separately that I ever shot and most weighed eight to nine pounds. The very biggest was a male, called a 'dog', which weighed twelve pounds. Anyway, for this fox to carry both chickens, minus wings and feet, was quite a feat.

My brother took the army rifle and watched that den for several hours, but no fox ever came out. It was probably sleeping off a nice meal of chicken.

Foxes are excellent mouse catchers and that is one, if not its greatest, source of food in this area. One day, a neighbor boy, took a shot at a fox and missed, but on the snow lay seven dead mice that the fox was carrying to her pups.

I have spent many winter hours trying to match wits with old Reynard and most times it won.

One of the strangest sounds I have ever heard is a fox barking. It sounds more like a squawk. If heard at night, it is a very scary sound.

Reynard is the fable and folklore name for the fox.

HAND CRANK TELEPHONE

~~~~~

In the 1940s, the party line and the hand crank telephone was what we had. We were on the R party line so everyone on our line had a telephone number that started with R. Pretty clever! Our number was R-20.

To call someone on your line you used a combination of long and short rings. This was accomplished by turning the crank on the right side of the wooden box which held all the parts, including the mouthpiece. The earpiece was on a cord, which was attached to the box. The phone was mounted on a wall and was a good sized affair. If I wanted to use the phone, I had to scoot a chair over and stand on it to reach the mouthpiece and turn the crank.

If someone wanted to call our house and they were on our line, they would ring three short rings. Other homes had one long and two shorts, etc. I think the possible combinations for up to three or four rings must be less than 20. That would be how many homes would be on your party line.

One real problem was trying to judge if the ring was a long or a short. Lyle's longs lasted four or five seconds. Others had a long that was just barely longer than a short. And then there were people whose shorts were longer than other people's longs. Sound confusing? It was. The general ring was four longs! This meant you were to pick up the phone and listen as the call was meant to inform the people on the line of something like 'my house is on fire, come quick'.
~~~~~

This happened on two occasions that I remember. Dad grabbed milk cans and filled them with water, put a ladder on the trailer and headed to the fire. In both cases, so many people arrived in such a short time, that they were able to quickly put the fire out. They didn't have much in the line of equipment, but they could get to the fire quickly. Of course, big fires, such as barns, were beyond the neighbor's ability to put out, but they could still help move animals and machinery. Today, trained volunteer firemen and 911 brings top notch help and equipment.

Another great use of the general call was for community announcements. Events at the Beaver Brook School could be announced by the phone. World War II was going on and if a mother received a letter from a son or daughter, it could be read to all on the line. Meeting reminders were sent that way also.

The one real drawback to the hand crank phone, and party line, was that if someone rang your house, the ring sounded in all the other homes on that line. So, if someone wanted to listen to what this call was about, you put your hand over the mouthpiece and lifted up the receiver and listened. This was called rubbernecking. There was no privacy on a party line whatsoever. Worse than that, there could be so much background noise, like barking dogs, doors slamming, etc. at some rubberneck's house that did not cover the mouthpiece, that you could not hear the person who called you. It was better than no phone, but just barely.

There was another advantage to those party lines and hand crank phones, more than two parties could talk on the line. In fact, if there was a meeting that needed to be held, pronto, you could ring all those on your line and start holding the meeting. Slick, huh?

Once I heard my mother talking to someone about an upcoming event involving the neighborhood. At one point they wondered if Bertha would be able to help. My mother said, "Let's ask her. Bertha, are you on the line?" Bertha was a notorious rubberneck and after a short pause replied that she was on the line. I was impressed!

Any calls late at night were sure to get everyone on the line. It must be something juicy to listen to. Most people would not conduct business on the phone because of the rubbernecks.

If you needed to call another party line you needed to call the operator by ringing one long ring. At a switchboard in Shell Lake, the operator would connect your party line with the one you requested and the operator rang the other party. Sometime in the late 1940s, the hand crank phones were replaced by a rotary phone. The party line remained for several more years. However, the phones did not ring in everyone's home. It got down to only three or four homes on a line.

My Mom grew up in Eau Claire, Wisconsin which is a city of around 60,000 now. She went back to visit for a week or so each summer and took us three ragamuffins along. Things sure seemed boring there. Too many houses and streets and too much visiting by the older people. One thing that my Grandpa had that was cool was a rotary phone. Where was the crank? It must have been progress starting in the city.

This is an interesting story my Dad told about early telephones. This took place about 1910 or thereabouts. Telephone lines were strung and most people in the community had a hand crank telephone.

One enterprising young man by the name of Raushsted got the idea of making the four long rings on the telephone. He then proceeded to play his violin for all who wanted to listen. Apparently it was a big hit and requests were made to do it again. My Dad said it was a forerunner of the radio, even though it was on the telephone.

THE GRATE

~~~~~

Our house was built in 1923 and was basically square. There were four large gables upstairs, with a bedroom in three of them and a bathroom in the fourth one. It had a large cast iron furnace in the basement, with a large grate right above it. This grate was located in the floor of the living room on the main floor.

From my first recollection, we burned coal for heat. There was a strike by the coal miners in the mid to late 1940s and Dad switched over to #2 fuel oil. My oldest brother dug a large hole just outside the south basement wall. Dad put a 500 gallon tank in the hole, covered it up and ordered fuel oil. Dad said he paid four cents per gallon the first time he filled it. Does that sound cheap?

Anyway, the heat came right up through that grate and in winter time this is where we all gathered, especially in the morning. There was only one heat run for the entire upstairs and that heated the bathroom and all the other rooms because it came out in the stairwell. Some heat got into the bedrooms, but just barely. In fact, in the real cold weather it was **darn cold** in my bedroom, which was the north one.

I had to load blankets on the bed to the point I could barely turn over. I learned to undress and put my clothes right beside the bed so I could slide my hand out, grab the clothes and shoes, count to three and jump out and run downstairs and get by the grate.
~~~~~

The grate worked good for drying clothes in the winter. Mom had a fold-up wooden rack that she put over the grate and hung clothes on that. It really worked. In the 1940s there were no clothes dryers that we knew about. If she wouldn't have put them over the grate, she would have had to hang them outside on the clothes line and that would have been difficult and very cold.

Houses in our neighborhood did not have air conditioners. We had several large box elder trees immediately south of the house so they kept the house fairly cool, but if needed, Dad would turn on the furnace fan and it brought up cool air from the basement, never mind that it smelled like a musty basement. At least it was cool.

HEALTH CARE

~~~~~

In the early 1940s, there was no hospital in Shell Lake. Doctors had office hours, but they also made house calls. My two younger brothers were born at home, as was my wife, and the doctor was called to assist with the delivery.

Many times I remember Dr. Dale came roaring into the yard, as he drove fast, and came into the house carrying his black bag. He had very good bedside manners and was a real friendly person. He would diagnose the problem, give pills, or recommend something, and then he was gone.

Finally about the mid 1940s a new, small hospital was built in Shell Lake. It also contained the clinic, but the entire building was small. About the time the new facility was built, I got a sinus infection. Dr. Dale's treatment was to take long Q-tip type sticks, soak them in some iodine looking brown liquid and stick them way up your nose, two sticks in each nostril. Then I had to lie down under a warm light for 10-15 minutes. It seemed like strange treatment, but it worked, or at least it seemed to.

What worked even better by that time was penicillin which showed up in the 1940s. It was administered with an injection in the buttocks and it hurt. It was hailed as a wonder drug and it sure seemed to be a cure all for nearly anything wrong with a person.

Polio reared its ugly head in the 1940s. Several kids in our area got sick with it. One of my classmates survived it, but her left arm was much thinner than her right. I don't recall
~~~~~

that anyone died around Shell Lake. This was about the time we heard of the Iron Lung. Sister Kenney, in the Twin Cities, was a name associated with treating polio.

Another thing that occurred was undulant fever which was caused by drinking raw cow's milk from cows with a disease called Bangs, or Brucellosis. Our school bus route started southeast of Shell Lake and continued east, etc. There was a family living about three miles from town and a couple kids rode the bus. For several days they didn't ride. Finally, someone went to their home and found several people were dead. I can't recall all the particulars, but all farm kid's lives changed. It was recommended that milk be pasteurized before drinking. Nearly everyone living in the country milked cows and drank the raw milk.

Immediately all cows were tested to see if they carried bangs. If they did, they had to be shipped to market. Many herds had cows with bangs. Testing was done periodically until no bangs was found. Wisconsin became 'bangs free' and that was a big deal.

Back to the milk at home. To pasteurize milk, it meant it had to be brought to within a whisker of the boiling point for a few seconds. This would kill any harmful bacteria in the milk. The problem is that to get a large kettle of milk heated up to just below the boiling point took time and you needed to be there to read the thermometer and take it off the heat at just the right moment. If it boiled, it tasted like boiled milk and I certainly didn't like it. Every once in a while we got the milk off the heat in time. Otherwise, we mixed chocolate syrup with it, or a little coffee if we were in a hurry. This went on for several years.

Once a week we had to take goiter pills. These pills were dispensed in school. They were little chocolate flavored pills and contained iodine. Students took turns passing out these great tasting pills and we were thrilled to be chosen to do it. Some of the boys were reported as sneaking back into the classroom and eating a couple extra pills. It is important to have proper levels of iodine in our bodies to prevent the development of a goiter, which is an enlargement of the thyroid in the throat area. As a kid, I recall several ladies with goiters. Today, children don't take these pills because the iodine is added to salt, called iodized salt.

Rheumatic fever was common in the 1940s as well. It follows some type of strep infection and affects the valves of the heart. Several kids got sick from it. One of my brothers contracted it and recovered from it, but could not participate in athletics until he was a sophomore in high school. One of my classmates was very sick and nearly died from it. She was out of school for several months. I don't recall anyone dying from rheumatic fever in the Shell Lake area.

Most of the young people got chicken pox and were out of school for a week or two. Boy, the pox would itch. We didn't think it was anything dangerous back then. Today, we realize chicken pox can be very dangerous and can have serious consequences if contracted later in life.

One day my neighbors, the Waldron's, had a little girl and her parents visiting them. I went to their house to meet them and walk to country school together. Here was this small, fragile girl with blue lips. She went to school with us that day. She walked slow and seemed to not have much energy.

This little girl was a Blue Baby. She apparently had a hole in her heart, and some blood got recirculated before it went to the lungs to get more oxygen. I don't think she had a very long life expectancy. Today that is a routine operation. Much has happened in the world of medicine. In my own case, I am on my third pacemaker. Lucky me! Thirty years earlier and you would not be reading these lines.

Something else from the good old days - cod liver oil. YUCK! It seemed like we got a spoonful once a day. It helped if you held your nose while taking it. Today the vitamin pill takes the place of cod liver oil. Also, from time to time, we got caster oil. Super Yuck! I don't even know what it was for except to make kids hate the stuff.

When the new hospital in Shell Lake opened, a private room was $5 per day and a double room was $4 per day. Today's medicine doesn't even deal with numbers that small. Dr. Dale made my Dad a deal about 1949. He would take out my tonsils and adenoids, along with my two younger brothers, for the price of two. That was three for the price of two! However, we would have to share a room. They put two beds together and we would have to lay crossways on them. My Dad took the deal and we got it done. We really liked getting all the ice cream they gave us.

This same doctor in Shell Lake examined eyes and prescribed glasses. All three of us wore glasses, as well as Mom and Dad. We also wore athletic glasses in high school. Our choices for frames were about as limited as our choice of cars in those days. Anyway, it worked. We did break many pairs and I lost at least one pair of glasses at the bottom of our neighbor's pond. Those glasses all had glass lenses and they were heavy. We had sore ears often from the tight fitting bows.

Later, I went through several pair of athletic glasses and my last pair has a big scratch on them from where a huge football player from Superior State, knocked my helmet off, along with my glasses. He then proceeded to step on them and scratch the lens. I did manage to block him even without my helmet. Looking back, I don't think that was very smart.

Penicillin was discovered in 1943. In 1944, one of my older brothers had an ear infection that spread to his brain and he was taken to a hospital in St. Paul, Minnesota. In order to save his life, the hospital used up its entire supply of penicillin at a cost of $50 per shot. It did save his life, but he could not talk or hear because of the seriousness of the infection.

THE GROCERY STORE

~~~~~

Life in the 1940s was vastly different than today. For one thing, World War II was fought from 1941 to 1945. Grocery shopping in Shell Lake was way different than today.

There was no supermarket, no shopping carts and no bright, cheery stores. In fact, the first thing in the store was a large, wide counter where all sales were transacted. My Dad did a lot of the shopping. He always had a list which he gave to the proprietor, or a helper. Because he was gone away from home during the day, he called Mom from the grocery store to get any last minute groceries. They proceeded to fill the order from the shelves in the store. Dad would go through the shelves, also, perhaps looking for some items that may not have made the list.

When all the items had been checked off, the bill was totaled and paid. Many people apparently had a weekly charge account. The groceries were put in empty boxes that were piled up behind the counter. Dad really liked mint patties, so that usually made the list. Dad frequently brought smoked salmon home. This was a snack food and must have been less expensive in comparison to today.

There were many of the same products we have today. Especially cereals, soaps, soup, canned vegetables and other canned foods. Fresh fruits and vegetables were also available. If we wanted fresh meat, we had to go to the meat market a few doors to the west.
~~~~~

The bakery was a few doors east and that is where we got bread, if it was needed. Mom baked bread, but it was hard to keep up with three growing boys who really liked peanut butter on fresh bread. Homogenizing was just being developed, so by the late 1940s we could buy peanut butter that was not separated with the oil going to the top. Previously you had to stir up the peanut butter and oil to mix the two together. It took awhile and even then you didn't mix it as well as the homogenized peanut butter we buy today.

Milk was also not homogenized and if it sat for a while the cream would rise to the top. If you liked, or needed cream, you could just skim it off. At school we got milk in glass half-pint jars and that cream would be on top. If you shook it up, the cream would mix with the milk. I preferred to poke the straw in, drink the milk and at the end get that good cream. Homogenizing is a process that breaks the fat (cream) into much smaller units so it does not rise to the top.

Also into the mix of buying groceries during the war were ration coupons. Certain items were in short supply and you could only purchase them if you had the proper ration coupon. The coupons came out once a month for each family. Coupons could be traded and that did happen. Some things that were rationed were sugar, rubber tires, gasoline, plus other things.

The last thing Dad would do before going home would be to visit the ice house and get a block of ice for the ice box. Refrigerators were not available during the war so we had the ice box.

It all worked out because that is the way it was years ago.

BROWN'S (TRADER'S) LAKE

~~~~~

About two miles from home is a small lake of about 40 acres that was all privately owned by a family named Trader. In my Dad's youth, that same lake was owned by the Brown's, hence the two names. It is flanked by hills on the east and west sides. During spring run off, water can come in from the south and go out the north and into a spring fed lake. This is the beginning of Beaver Brook.

The first time I ever went to this lake was during third or fourth grade at the Beaver Brook School. It was a school event that may have lasted all day. We all brought fishing poles and lunches. We left from school and walked to the railroad tracks. We then walked down the tracks to the lake. This was a small group of about ten kids and our teacher. I really don't know how we got the day off from school. We may have lobbied hard for it, or perhaps it was something that most country schools were doing. Anyway, it was loads of fun.

My fishing pole was a cane pole about 12 feet long. I had dug angle worms and was ready. One of the older girls fished with me and looked after me. I remember that we caught sunfish and had a great time.

This is a beautiful lake with sloping shorelines on the north end of the lake. As I stood watching my bobber, I looked in the water and here came a black blob, about two feet in diameter.

It slowly moved along the edge of the lake towards me. It
~~~~~

appeared to be made up of dozens of small fishlike critters. Finally, it was right by me so I knelt down and swatted into the blob hoping to splash one or two up on shore. I really could not tell what they were. I swatted and OUCH! I had three of them stuck to my hand. They were baby bullheads and their dorsal spines punctured my hand. I pulled them off and returned them to their brothers and sisters. At that point, I don't think I even knew there was such a fish as a bullhead. Many years later I saw the same kind of school of baby bullheads, but this time there was a large bullhead in the school, possibly their mother.

Over the next several years, many of us fished that lake and had good luck. Mostly pan fish, but we did catch some nice northern pike and one day fishing from a boat with my girl friend, Betty and her father, I caught three beautiful large mouth bass.

Another family lived near us and we fished together a few times. One day a train came by, so we decided to run up the hill and watch it. Up we went but someone stepped on a wasp nest in the ground. A little boy about 8 happened to be right behind and he got stung about ten or twelve times. He was in great pain and he was really crying. We took him back down to the lake and put mud on each bee sting. Amazingly, within a few minutes the swelling had all gone away and the little guy claimed the sting was mostly gone. Good thinking.

Another family fished often and at a 4-H meeting they told of catching all these nice northern pike by using frogs. They invited me to go with them the next morning at Oh Dark Thirty and I accepted.

I drove to their place and picked them up. If I remember correctly there were at least four kids. We drove across one of their fields and I ran over a small stump and we all hit the roof of the car. We walked to the lake using flashlights. We caught a few frogs, rigged them up and cast them out into a bed of lily pads and just left them for several minutes. No bobbers were used. From time to time, we checked to see if there was anything on the line. Several times there were fish. We caught several nice two to four pound northern. I have many pleasant memories of this lake. Unfortunately, when the new U. S. Highway 53 became a four lane road it was put in so close to this lake that heavy rains caused a large amount of mud to run into the lake. This killed all the fish and restocking has begun.

THE BLACKSMITH

~~~~~~

Joel was the blacksmith in Shell Lake. That certainly was the correct name because Joel was always covered with soot. He was a large man, somewhat robust and always had a pair of goggles up on his head. I am pretty sure he also chewed snoose.

He had the coolest shop. There was always a lot of iron laying around. Parts that needed welding or brazing were everywhere. There was a path through all of this and the most interesting thing for me was the forge. There always was a fire in the coals and if you turned the handle to pump air into the coals, they responded and it got very hot. Hot enough to melt iron and other metals.

His shop was quite old. He had an arc welder and some electric tools, but he also had a big overhead jack shaft that could power various pieces of equipment. One was a device that flattened metal by pounding on it. He had a metal saw, buffers, grinders and drills that ran off that one big shaft. He had to slide flat belts into position to make the equipment work. I think the shaft ran all the time and when he wanted to use something, he would slide the belt and it began working.

Before arc welders, iron was welded by heating two pieces until they were red hot and then they were pounded together. Joel could do that. He also apparently made horse shoes, although I don't recall that he shod horses. Apparently many blacksmiths did though.

Dad was a frequent visitor to the blacksmith shop. He was
~~~~~~

real good about taking us three ragamuffins to town with him. Perhaps Mom convinced him she needed some time without us. If so, I don't blame her one bit. Dad had done quite a bit of blacksmithing earlier and Joel would let him use the equipment to do whatever Dad was working on.

Dad and Joel got along very well. Dad was an inventor of sorts, so he was always making parts, modifying something or fixing something that broke. Joel kept an eye on us kids and he would let us know if we were doing something we should not be doing.

This was 'fix it' headquarters so there were various machines sitting around waiting to be fixed. When Dad could do his own work, Joel didn't mind at all.

On the south side of the blacksmith shop building was another shop of sorts. An old veterinarian headquartered there. I don't know if he ever had been trained, but farmers called him and he came out to treat milk fever, pull calves and other things. He was pretty laid back.

If we came to the blacksmith shop from the south, we walked through the vet's portion of the shop. Sometimes there would be a few older men sitting around chewing the fat.

The vet was also a gunsmith and he had a few guns for sale. When I was between sixth and seventh grade, we walked through the veterinarian room on our way to the blacksmith shop, and I saw a single shot shotgun in his rack with a price of $7.00. Dad went to see Joel and I asked about the shotgun. The vet handed the gun to me. It was an Iver Johnson 12 gauge with a full choke. There was no recoil pad and the vet told me, "It will kick like a mule." He was certainly right. Anyway, I convinced Dad to let me buy it. We stopped and got some high brass, 6 shot shotgun shells for twelve cents each.

I took the gun home and could hardly wait to shoot it. We picked out a target and Dad said, "Hold it real tight against your shoulder." I did that, pulled the trigger and **Holy Cow! It just about knocked me down!** I thought there is no way I could get used to shooting that gun. Dad was laughing and I was rubbing my sore shoulder.

Needless to say, I didn't do anything with that shotgun for many days. But eventually I could hear crows out in our woods and there was a bounty of 25 cents per crow head, so I took my gun, some shells and a folded up towel to protect my shoulder and I went hunting crows.

For your information, crows are a very tough adversary. They must have been able to see me leave the house. I could hear them, so I sneaked up on them, or at least I thought I did. I finally got a shot at one crow after several days. I put the folded up towel on my shoulder, put the gun against it and fired at a crow. At least I did not get knocked down, and the towel definitely cushioned the recoil. I missed the crow, but now I felt more confident.

Getting back to the veterinarian. Dad called him because he had a cow down with milk fever. This can happen when a cow has a calf and she begins to produce milk. This makes a shortage of calcium in the cow's blood and she goes down and can't get back up.

In the 1940s, the treatment that the vet performed was to take a hand tire pump with a needle on it, like you would use to pump up a football. He inserted the needle in the opening of a teat and pumped a bunch of air into that quarter of the udder. He then took a strip of cloth and tied up the end of the teat so the air didn't leak back out. He did that to all four quarters. I was thinking, what kind of a quack is this? In a few minutes, however, the cow got up and went about her business. That shows you what I knew about treating milk fever.

SNAKES

~~~~~

Just the name snakes, sounds scary to me. As a kid, we saw many snakes, many more than today. By far the most common was the garter snake. We had a silo pit that was loaded with snakes. They must have fallen in. Our dog, Laddie, grabbed a good sized garter snake one day and began shaking it. All of a sudden, there were many baby snakes flying through the air. They were four to five inches long and they were alive. I think Laddie killed the mother and perhaps the little ones survived. I have no way of knowing what happened to them.

We had water moccasins, or at least that is what we called them. They were in Beaver Brook and Brown's Lake as well as other places. They got to be about three feet long and could scare you. Several times while trout fishing, I was scared by the sudden appearance of a snake, either swimming on the bottom of a pool or at the top. More than once, I took my trout rod apart and headed home after seeing a good size water snake.

Pine snakes were the other big snakes we had around here. They could get up to four or five feet long and sometimes longer. They also could climb trees, buildings, etc. I once walked into a picnic shelter and there was a big pine snake stretched out on a beam. Good bye! I never saw very many pine snakes when I was a kid, maybe a dozen.

We had green grass snakes, too, that were garter snake size. We also had red bellied snakes. They are very small and are brown. They get very active at dusk. We heard rumors of
~~~~~

snow snakes and hoop snakes, but I think we can thank Paul Bunyan for those rumors.

By far the most interesting snake we had was the hog-nosed snake. We called them blow snakes, while some people called them puffer snakes. I have seen quite a large number of these. They only get two to three feet long, but sometimes longer. They may coil up and flair out their neck and hiss like crazy if they are scared. The first time I ever saw that was at a time when my friend Jerry and I had just finished fishing on Brown's Lake and had climbed up the hill to the railroad track. About that time a train came along so we put down our fish poles and tackle boxes to watch the train. The engine came about the time we put our stuff down. But even with all the noise we heard a loud hissing sound.

We looked down and between us was a big hog-nosed snake, coiled up and hissing. We probably set a new record for the standing jump, at least for height. We ran away and noticed the engineer looking at us. He probably thought we were crazy. Anyway, long after the train had passed, we found clubs for each of us and went to beat the shrubbery on the way to get our poles and tackle boxes. We were relieved to get out of there.

Other things I have seen them do after they try to scare you by hissing, is they will play dead. They bleed out of their eyes and will vomit and roll on their back or side.

They are very strong and their hog nose is perfect for rooting under branches, leaves and maybe stones.

Apparently there are rattle snakes around too, but I have

never seen one. There is a snake called a horse hair snake. I found one once in a small swamp on our farm at home. They are very long and are very thin, about as thick as a toothpick. They are really not snakes, but they are alive.

On two occasions, I heard high pitched screaming coming from the grass. Investigating, I found that a garter snake had caught a frog and the frog was screaming. In both cases, the snake had caught the frog at right angles at its stomach. It took a few minutes, but the snake slowly rotated the frog around so it could swallow it head first, which it finally did in both cases. I felt sorry for the frog, but I did not interfere.

HOT WHEELS

~~~~~~

When I was in the second grade, I got about the best present I had ever received for any Christmas. A BIKE! It was a full sized, boys bike. It still had snow on it, so Santa must have just been there. I did not care that it was used, it was MY BIKE!

In second grade, I was not very big and that full sized bike was a bit much. I did not care. I had never ridden a bike before, but I sure envied kids that had one.

I put my outside clothes on and took my bike out and tried to ride it down our driveway which was fairly steep. I could barely touch the pedals, in fact, I had to rock from side to side in order to keep my feet on the pedals.

You can probably guess that I crashed and burned **dozens of times** that day. Out of at least a hundred tries, I managed to ride 20-30 feet maybe three or four times. But, boy I was happy! I don't know if training wheels had been invented yet. They sure weren't in our neighborhood.

In the next few days I got so I could ride. The snow covered roads were treacherous, but I rode around our place, but not on to the highway. But I hoped by spring I could go on County Road B and maybe U. S. Highway 53. However, those big trucks were very scary.

Spring arrived, and the road past our house was a dirt road, which meant a muddy road for many days. Riding my bike was nearly impossible. That was alright because we had all
~~~~~~

this running water to play in. I had just studied about the Zuider Zee in Holland so I built several dikes on the edge of the road past our house.

Eventually, the mud dried up and I got my bike out again. I just loved riding that bike. I was content to ride back and forth past our driveway. I would go to County Road B, turn around and go to U. S. Highway 53. This was about a quarter of a mile. Eventually, I rode a little way on County Road B before I turned around. I did the same thing on U. S. Highway 53.

One day, I asked Mom and Dad if I could ride up to Hall's driveway on County Road B. Dad said I would have to wait until he could follow me with the car. He told me I had to always ride on the right side of the road. I had to be real careful and not take any chances.

The day finally arrived when Dad could follow me, so off we went. Boy, I was nervous. Hall's driveway was about a quarter mile from the end of the road past our place. It went just fine. It sure was swell, riding on the blacktop, nice and smooth. After that, I was allowed to go to Hall's driveway by myself. That was fine, but . . .I wanted to go farther and maybe go on U. S. Highway 53. Once in awhile, a big semi came by and they were scary.

Eventually, I was allowed to go on U. S. Highway 53, too. When a semi came in my lane, I drove down off the edge of the road - right down in the ditch.

I eventually got to ride to school and as time went on, I didn't have any restrictions as to where I could go. One day, when I was in third grade, several of the boys from the Beaver Brook School met near the track hill. This was a fairly steep hill on County Road B that ran east of the railroad tracks. It was decided that we should race down this hill. I was the youngest and three or four boys were big old sixth, seventh and eighth graders. But, off we went. I had to pedal standing up, as I could still not reach the pedals if I was sitting. I jumped into an early lead. Boy, I was flying! Then disaster struck. One of my feet slipped off the pedal and my crotch fell on the bar that makes a bike a boys bike and that really hurt! It hurt so much that I could not keep the bike on the road and I went right into a little swamp and tipped over. I was a mess, all wet and covered with swamp weeds and mud. However, the pain in my crotch had improved. Oh, well, live and learn.

Another thing you always had to do was roll up your pant leg on the side where the chain was. My bike did not have a chain guard, at least it didn't have one when it was mine. Failure to roll up your pant leg would eventually result in your pant leg getting caught in the sprocket for the chain. At the very least, your pants leg got greasy. More often, the sprocket poked some holes in the pant leg.

Bikes needed a lot of tinkering. You had to get the wheels to run straight. The chain always needed adjustment for tension and the tires needed air. The handle bars and seat needed constant adjusting to get the maximum speed and comfort. This was my first contact with wrenches. I enjoyed the tinkering, but I enjoyed riding even more.

I learned how to ride 'no hands'. I also learned that when

you rode on wet or muddy roads, you got a stripe up your back and splattered up in front.

By the fourth grade, I made a deal to buy a bike frame, no wheels, from one of the kids at school. I think he sold it to me for $5.00 which was high, but it had a coil spring on the front fork. It was painted a light blue.

I took the wheels off my old bike and put them on the new frame. That coil spring really made a difference riding on 'washboard roads'. I could really fly. I was bigger now, and when I reached down and held the lower pipe, I could really give it. I could beat all the kids that were in school. There were about ten besides me and about half of them were girls. One girl, Delores, was an eighth grader and she was next fastest and boy she could really hit a softball, too.

I rode my bike until I could drive the car, which was about age fifteen. I learned to carry a lot of different things on my bike, like baseball glove and bat, shotgun and .22 rifle, fishing pole, tackle box, creel, extra clothes and if lucky, a partridge or two, crows for bounty, fish, like the big eighteen inch northern I caught for my first legal northern. Eighteen inches was the minimum length and it sure looked big to me.

One day I was going past the Badger Cranberry Marsh and I saw that there were some people living in one of the small buildings used by some workers during the harvest. I stopped and talked to them and saw they were both Indians. A lady in her twenties and a man about that same age. They were friendly and apparently were hired, or at least the man was, to work around the marsh. I had my .22 single shot rifle with me on the bike. The man was interested in it and wanted to hold it. I let him. The man mentioned something about riding in a box car recently. Maybe they were hobos. They did seem like decent, nice people, however.

I told my Mom and Dad about meeting them and they were really upset that I had done that and told me not to go back again. This really surprised me. My parents were generally not judgmental that I know of. Perhaps they were fearful that they may harm me. After all, they were transients.

THE WAR AND A SMALL BOY

~~~~~

When Japanese planes attacked Pearl Harbor on December 7, 1941, I was a three year old boy living with my parents and three brothers on a small dairy farm in northern Wisconsin. Our daily life was quiet and peaceful. When news of the bombing reached rural Shell Lake, the town we lived near, I learned a new word - WAR. From that day on our lives would change in many subtle ways, ultimately affecting the very fiber of our souls.

As a three year old boy, however, I wasn't too concerned with that thing the big people called 'war'. I could tell it was serious though because the adults always talked in hushed voices and shook their heads a lot. I didn't understand just what had happened in that far away place called Pearl Harbor, but I knew it was bad. I heard my Dad talking about airplanes and ships and men as well as women dying. It was scary and exciting at the same time.

Our day to day life, for the most part, continued at much the same gentle pace, but gradually our small community, as were all others, was drawn into the great global conflict. Many young men went off to war and many other people left to build ships, planes, tanks and other war materials. We would all do whatever we could to help our brave troops.

Adults huddled around radios to hear the latest developments in the war. Newspapers and magazines covering the war were eagerly read. Our lives, however, did go on within the ever present shadow of the war.
~~~~~

The early years of the war impacted our family in a unique way. My Mother's brother, Earl and his wife, Louise, were missionaries living with their two young sons in the Philippines. This was one of the very first places where Japanese and American soldiers fought each other and very little information about Earl and Louise and the boys reached us during the war. We learned the youngest son, Earl Douglas, who was my age, was living with his parents as they fled the Japanese. Their oldest son, Donal, was thought to be fighting with Philippine Guerillas against the Japanese. We later learned that he had been attending school in Manila and had been captured by the Japanese. He was held with other Americans in a prison camp in Manila. He was able to continue his studies, but like many prisoners, he contracted Beri Beri. The return of the U. S. troops saved his life as he felt he could only survive a few more weeks when they were liberated. The Bataan Death March in the Philippines was one of the first images I had of the human suffering of the war.

We had no television in 1941, so our knowledge of the war came from the radio, our daily newspaper from Superior, Wisconsin, and magazines such as the *Saturday Evening Post* and *Life*. My Mother and Dad were both teachers and they read to us until we were old enough to read for ourselves. They tried to explain what the war was about, where it was and especially any news of the Philippines. Once in a while, we would go to a movie and there we would see newsreels of the war. These were graphic battle scenes with lots of explosions, planes flying, sea battles and a lot of smoke. These really impressed me as to how horrible war was and how dangerous it was for our servicemen. I was thankful that all this fighting was not near my home, but I did feel sorry for kids and people who lived where the war was being fought. I could imagine the terror that the kids felt as bombs, etc. blew up and destroyed their homes and lives.

News of war events were also spread by word of mouth. In the 1940s, men of the community worked together frequently to build barns, thresh grain, fill the silo and cut wood. As small kids, we were allowed to be around the men. During breaks, the talk of war occupied their discussions with stories about battles, weapons, strategy, local service men and women and the impact locally that the war had on their lives.

As time went on, and the United States was helping the allies fight the Nazi's in Europe, the impact of the war became more intense. Each family was given coupon books to allow only limited purchases of sugar, gasoline, rubber tires and other items. This did work hardships on families from time to time. I can remember my mother trading coupons with neighbors to try to get needed supplies for our family of seven people, as another brother was born in 1942. Each family raised a 'Victory Garden', filled with all types of vegetables and all available food would be sent to 'our boys overseas'. In some cases, golf courses were plowed up and vegetables planted to be sure our troops were well supplied with food.

ROSIE, THE RIVETER posters appeared which showed Rosie dressed in coveralls and holding a rivet gun implying that it was alright for women to build ships, planes, etc. and their help was needed now. Posters of Uncle Sam were everywhere also. He was pointing a finger and saying, "I WANT YOU." I took this to mean that I was needed just like everyone else. We were beginning to realize that we all had to do whatever we could to help the war effort. War bond drives were very popular and well supported. People would buy these bonds to help finance our war effort. As kids, we were encouraged to contribute toward bonds that our family purchased.

As small kids, we searched our families' dump site, and other places, for scrap iron, aluminum, copper, brass and tin cans. We also collected paper and rags which were sold for a small amount of cash. We felt that we were doing our part to 'help our boys overseas'. The school kids all had tin foil balls which we got by peeling foil from gum wrappers, cigarette packages and candy wrappers. A big tin foil ball was a status symbol for us, however, eventually we would sell them for a few pennies to help the war effort. In the fall we got time off from country school to pick milkweed pods. These pods were full of fuzzy seeds that were to be used in fliers jackets. Helping to do our part for the war effort made my friends and me feel important.

The war did not affect many things in my life such as going to school, playing with my brothers and friends, or doing chores on our farm. We would explore the woods around our place, swim in a neighbor's pond, and go sliding and skiing in the winter with other kids. I was in awe of the birds and animals around us and enjoyed spring when birds returned and things began to grow again. Winters were fun for kids, but they got long. Summer time meant bare feet, short hair cuts and long lazy afternoons to read or just lay under a tree and talk with my brothers or friends.

Mom and Dad tried to explain what the war was all about, but at that time it seemed quite complicated to me. They also explained why certain people were drafted and some volunteered to go to war. It was hard for me to understand why countries would hate each other enough to make war.

As the war progressed and I got old enough to at least look at pictures of the war in the *Saturday Evening Post* and *Life* magazines, we often saw 'Kilroy was Here' scrawled on buildings, etc., by our troops in lighter moments. War correspondents like Ernie Pyle traveled with the troops affectionately called 'Dog Faces' and wrote about how our troops fought, lived and died. Many people back home admired his work.

I remember how sad I was to learn that he had been killed in the battle for Okinawa near the end of the war. He was a special person to me even though he was not a soldier. He was an important link between our troops and the folks back home. Ernie Pyle was a gifted writer and was admired by the troops with whom he traveled.

Growing up in the shadow of the war, many names became synonymous with the war. There were good guys and bad guys. These characters loomed larger than life to a four or five year old. The good guys were our brave American Officers. Well known and respected for their tough jobs were men like Eisenhower, Patton, MacArthur, Nimitz, Bradley and many more. Allied names were Montgomery from England and DeGaulle from France. The bad guys were Tojo, Hirohito and Tokyo Rose. The Germans were Hitler, of course, Rommel, Goering and others. World leaders we heard about were Franklin D. Roosevelt from the USA and Winston Churchill from England. These men were symbols of peace in a world craving for peace. Late in the war, Roosevelt died and Harry Truman was the new President of the United States.

As small kids we knew all the service songs and sang them often. We played war games using sticks for guns. We wallowed in the mud after seeing a newsreel of our soldiers doing that. We would comb our hair off to the side and hold a comb under our nose to look like Hitler. This was great fun as a child! In retrospect, as an adult, this speaks to the macabre nature of the era, and leaves me feeling unsettled.

Richard Bong was the American 'Ace of Aces' and grew up at Poplar, Wisconsin which was not too far from our home. He was a real hero to us all. His exploits in his P-38 Lightning were appearing regularly in our daily paper and he was credited with shooting down 40 Japanese planes. He was killed, not in the war but as a test pilot for Jet planes near the end of the war. We were all very sad and it just did not seem fair to me.

Macarthur's 'I will Return' was one of the big statements of the war. He made this statement as the Japanese drove him off the Bataan Peninsula in the Philippines at the start of the war. He did return later and liberated the Philippines. One of the most famous pictures of the war was the flag raising on Mt. Subiachi on Iwo Jima. One of the flag raisers was John Bradley from Antigo, Wisconsin, who I personally became acquainted with later in my life. I coached two of his sons in football, but John was always reluctant to talk about his role in that famous picture. This picture became a national symbol for freedom. One of the biggest thrills in my life was to be able to visit the two immense monuments of the raising the flag on Iwo Jima. One monument is located near Arlington National Cemetery in Washington, D. C. and the other is at Harlingen, Texas.

B-24 bombers were built in St. Paul, Minnesota and these planes were test flown and their guns tested over Lake Superior. On their way back to St. Paul, many of the planes flew so low over our house that we could see the pilots. We lived near U. S. Highway 53 and I saw several blue buses that carried both Japanese and German Prisoners of War (POW's). At the time, we thought they were on their way to work on the Iron range in northern Minnesota, but later I learned that some of the German POW's had worked on farms near us. One farmer said that most of the German POW's who worked for him were hard working, nice guys. The SS trained POW's however, were very aloof and claimed that Germans were a superior race and would win this war.

Many people from our area worked at the ship yards in Superior, Wisconsin and many wives were left at home to carry on while their husbands built ships, planes, etc. Iron ore trains ran on railroad tracks located a short distance from our place to keep up with the demand for steel. These were long, slow moving trains requiring two 'pusher' engines to get up a long grade near our home. These were a great fascination to small kids and we would go and watch them whenever possible.

Our community was drawn together as we all did what we could to help our men and women over-seas. The hand crank telephone was used to tell of important meetings and news of servicemen in our community. As these were party lines, four long rings alerted the fifteen or so families on the line to pick up the phone and hear the news. Any servicemen home on leave were treated like hero's.

In 1944, one of my older brothers, age 12, suffered an ear infection which spread to his brain. He was rushed to a hospital in St. Paul and an operation was performed, but the doctors said the infection had spread too far. A new wonder drug, penicillin, had just become available for $50 per shot. A series of these shots could save his life, but he would not be able to talk or hear. Of course, my parents chose to use the penicillin and eventually he came home. Times were very trying for the entire family. With the war in progress there was so much uncertainty and with my brother being so sick it was an extremely difficult time for the entire family.

Late in the war, by now I was about seven years old, word came that one of our relatives, Hugh Miller, had been killed. He was a fighter pilot and was shot down over France. Hugh was a real hero and had died fighting for our country. Our little town and surrounding community was saddened and we were left with an empty feeling that one of our finest young men would not return to us.

The Big Battles were in the news: Midway, Iwo Jima, Okinowa, D-Day, Battle of the Bulge and many others. We learned a lot about world geography by finding these places on a globe or on the map. My parents tried to explain what the strategy was for troop deployment and supply shipments by ships, etc.

As the war was nearing its end, my mother received word that her brother, his wife and their youngest son were captured and killed by the Japanese. Earl and Louise were beheaded and Earl Douglas, who was the same age as me, was bayoneted, or stabbed with a knife on the end of a rifle. My reaction to this news was poor Earl Douglas would not run and play anymore and I was sad for him.

This made a tremendous impact on our family and great sadness to my mother. She cried for many days. In the following days, my mother's family gathered at her parent's home in Eau Claire, Wisconsin to console each other and to attend a memorial service at a Baptist Church in Eau Claire. Earl and his family were missionaries from the Baptist Church and to this day a picture of Earl and his family still hangs in the church. I was beginning to get an idea about what death was and I did not like it.

On a warm August afternoon in 1945 we could hear a car honking in the distance. It came closer and eventually came past our home. The driver, Chuck, waved and shouted, "The War is Over, The War is Over!" Mom and Dad grabbed each other and did a little dance in our front yard. That was very exciting news and the country was at peace once again.

Like that warm August day, the summer was coming to an end and so was our country's great struggle to restore peace in the world. There was unbelievable happiness and relief as our brave troops returned home. Americans began to return to a world without war. Our efforts back home to support our troops made us all very proud to be Americans.

My life would continue without the influence of the war and I was grateful for that. The war was behind us, but all of our lives were forever changed.

SNOWY ROBINS

~~~~~~

One spring day in 1945, we had hundreds of robins around the yard. There were many times more robins than normal. This would have been close to the end of March or the first week of April and there were robins everywhere. Then a huge snowstorm hit. At least a foot of snow fell and the robins didn't seem to know what to do. I remember that a few days later, on the south side of our front porch, there were close to 200 robins all huddled together. I could go and stand by the edge of the porch and they did not fly away.

Mom and Dad came and looked, too. It was very sad as it looked like they would all die as some already looked weak. I wanted to feed them. We tried bread crumbs. It may have worked a little bit, but in the end many, but not all, died. The snow melted and the robins could find food. We found hundreds of dead robins that spring. Sometimes Mother Nature is cruel.

I really liked the robins. They are early returning birds and busy 'singing off' their territory and building nests. How they can catch worms escapes me. I have seen three batches of babies raised out of the same nest in one summer.

Other winter birds were snow buntings. These small white birds come in flocks and don't stay very long. Another is the horned lark. They stay longer than the snow buntings, but not all winter.

No one in our neighborhood fed bird seed in the 1940s. I know that people put out fat from butchering a steer. Also
~~~~~~

bones with meat scraps were put out for birds. But compared to the bird feeding of today, we didn't feed them.

Other birds in the winter were chickadees, nuthatches, blue jays, English sparrows, starlings and an occasional mourning dove.

Sometime in the late 1940s, it was early winter and I had been hunting with my shotgun and I was almost home. I saw the tracks of a relatively large bird in the snow. I followed the tracks and up jumped a large bird with a long tail. I thought it was a pheasant, which were very scarce in Northwest Wisconsin. I made a lucky shot and down it went. I ran up to it and saw it was a hen pheasant. They are strictly protected and it is illegal to kill one. Now what? I took it home, dressed it, Mom cooked it and we ate it. I did get a good lecture on not breaking laws, even game laws.

I felt extremely bad about shooting that hen pheasant, but not so bad that I wanted to go turn myself in to a game warden. I did, however, have a plan. I belonged to 4-H and one of the projects was to raise pheasants, so I thought this might be some repentance. I signed up to get pheasant eggs, which came from the state game farm at Poynette, Wisconsin. Sometime in May, a box with 106 brown speckled eggs was delivered to our place. We had made arrangements to get them hatched at the hatchery in Rice Lake, Wisconsin. Sometime later, 56 little fluff balls hatched out and we took them home. I had made a small pen near our house. It was made of half-inch chicken wire. It had a chicken wire fence over the top to keep out hawks, owls and other flying predators. There was a shelter in one corner. We thought we were ready.

We put the box in the pen, opened it and started lifting chicks out. Now these chicks are small. You could put one in your hand and close your fingers over the chick. Anyway, we got them all out of the box. Some had even found the food when Laddie, our dog came up and said, 'WOOF'. All 56 chicks ran through the half inch wire like it wasn't there.

We got Laddie locked up and then started looking for the chicks. Some had already come back in. We carefully went around the edge and actually got all 56 back in their pen. We took window screens and put them in until I could get smaller screen.

The little chicks grew rapidly. We had to put permanganate in the water and we got big bones from the butcher for them to peck at. One night a skunk burrowed under and killed about 25 of them. We dug the fence down and that prevented any more losses in that manner.

By now they were developing tail feathers. But these pheasants were bound and determined to pull out each other's tail feathers. Finally, I opened the gate and let them out in late August. These beautiful birds sure looked strange without their long tail feathers. I saw them several times, but eventually they flew away and I never saw them again. At least I felt better about shooting the hen the winter before.

THE WONDERFUL CHOCOLATE

~~~~~

One morning, my Dad was milking the cows and I strolled in. I was barefooted with my bibbed overalls on. This was in 1943 and I was five years old. He wanted me to go to the house and get some medicine for a cow. I had to look on the top shelf of the cupboard by the sink to get some medicine that was there.

Off I went. I had to climb up and stand on the cabinet and then I could just barely peek over the shelf. I could not find the medicine Dad wanted. I did find a little flat box that I was curious about. I opened it and found little flat pieces of chocolate. Of course, I ate some. I looked again, still no medicine, so I went out and told Dad I could not find the medicine. He explained it again and told me to go in and look another time.

Hooray!! I could get another piece or two of that nice flat chocolate candy. I climbed up, took a couple pieces, and looked again for that medicine.

About that time, my Mother came in and wanted to know what I was doing on the cabinet. I told her that I was trying to get medicine for Dad, but I couldn't find it. She looked in the cupboard and found it. She also found the X-Lax box was nearly empty and asked if I knew anything about that. I didn't know. But Mom knew! I finally told her how many pieces I ate and she was scared. She immediately called the doctor wondering how serious this might be. The doctor told Mom, "Oh, he will be alright. He will be a busy little boy today, however." I was busy and I don't remember if Dad ever got the medicine or not.
~~~~~

About the next year, I had started first grade at Beaver Brook and really liked school. I would walk home with two different groups of kids. One group going down County Road B and the other going on U. S. Highway 53. Our road connected the two highways.

Mom, and sometimes Dad, would be home when I got home from school. If they could not be home, arrangements were made for me to go to one of the other kid's house and they would pick me up later.

One day I got home and nobody was there!! I was scared. I searched the house, barn and other buildings and finally went in to lie down on the grate because it was warm there. I felt safe in that familiar place. When you listen, there are all kinds of little noises that a house makes due to a variety of reasons. I heard every one of them. The longer I was there, the more scared I got. Where were Mom and Dad? Did something happen to them? What about my two brothers? Maybe there was an accident. I am sure Mom didn't tell me to go to someone else's house.

Finally, I cried. Not loud. I wouldn't want whoever is upstairs to hear me. Now my imagination was running wild. Is that someone coming down the stairs? Did someone just peek in the window at me? What was that scratching I hear? Finally, I fell asleep. I don't know how long I slept, but I woke up when my Mom and Dad and two brothers came home and found me. They had gone to Rice Lake and had had car trouble. Boy, was I glad to see them! I guess I wasn't very brave after all.

PAINTING THE BARN

~~~~~

Dad built a new barn in 1942. At least that is when it got finished. Work began several years earlier by cutting the logs in our woods and getting them sawed into lumber. The barn was eighty feet long, 30 feet wide and 36 feet high. It takes a lot of lumber to build a barn of that size.

Footings for the foundation were dug by hand. Rocks were hauled in to fill up the trench to make footings. The short walls of the barn were formed up and concrete was mixed by hand and wheeled over to the forms. Finally, the lower part of the barn was built in 1941, some hay was put on top to insulate it for the winter months. The summer of 1942 came along, the large round roof rafters were cut and nailed together. These boards were oak, maple and basswood. The oak and maple needed to be drilled because they were so hard.

Finally the rafters were raised. Many neighbors helped and by the end of the day all the rafters were up. But, a big windstorm came up later that evening and blew all the rafters down. I remember seeing the roof from another building go blowing by our house. It was pretty scary.

After the storm passed, the neighbors came to see the mess. Insurance covered most of the loss and work began to rebuild the rafters. Actually most of the rafters were really not hurt too badly. Anyway, the barn got built by the summer of 1942.

The barn received its first coat of paint in 1943 and I did not help with that.
~~~~~

In 1950, Dad decided the barn needed a second coat of paint. That would be the main project for the summer. Dad made it clear that the three of us boys would be expected to help. Painting is an easy job - to put off. Remember, I was only 12 years old and my brothers were two and four years younger.

We got started. Dad bought paint in five gallon pails. The bottom six or eight boards were painted gray and the rest of the barn was white. The side walls were not bad, especially the north side because it was in the shade.

Finally, we had to do the ends. Dad had made an extension ladder that would reach the peak, 36 feet off the ground. This meant the ladder was made up of two - twenty foot long sections and weighed a little less than a Packard. To raise that ladder took all three of us kids, plus Dad. We would get it set for the right height and put the bottom of the ladder against the barn. We then lifted it up and began 'walking' it higher and higher. As we did this, there was more and more weight behind us, so Dad had rigged a 'pike pole' type of deal to reach up with the pole and push also. When the ladder was straight up we had to pull the base out a few feet.

With the ladder in place, we could go up and start painting. Maybe we better eat lunch first. Anything to stall on starting to paint the barn.

Finally, we had to do it. Since I was the oldest, it was my duty to go up and paint. At least that is what the other two brothers thought. I took a paint pail and brush and started up this tall ladder. At that age I really didn't mind high places, but at 36 feet, that was up there. I started swabbing the paint, really concentrating on my job at hand. Reaching up and out to paint the soffet was no fun. I had been up there for about an hour when, all of a sudden, one brother grabbed the ladder, shook it and hollered, "How are you doing up there?" Needless to say, I dropped the pail of paint and the brush. I held on tight to the ladder. I was scared. The last laugh was on him because as the paint pail fell it landed in just the right way so the paint shot out and sprayed him as he was running away. He was covered with paint on his backside. It served him right. I certainly was not real anxious to go up that ladder again. Oh, by the way, neither was my brother as long as I was around. I guess he thought I might want to get even. Think so?? We had other ladders which were eventually all nicely speckled with white paint.

My Dad use to say, "One boy is a boy, two boys is half a boy and three boys is no boy at all!" We knew he was right. He also used to say, "Ernie gets more work out of his two girls than I get out of you three boys." We knew he was right about that also. I married one of those girls and she is wonderful and she is a worker.

We finally did get the barn painted that summer.

THE HAY BUCKEROO

~~~~~

My Dad was always building something new, or modifying other equipment and the Hay Buckeroo was one of these. About 1946, Dad got the idea to build this big scoop affair for the front of the tractor. He had seen where they were quite popular in many of the western states. Hay would be scooped up by driving the hay buckeroo down a windrow of hay. This continued until the buckeroo got filled. It was then taken to the haystack and somehow unloaded. There was a 'stacker' that picked up the hay and put it on the stack that was being built.

Dad must have thought that was pretty cool, so he started making a hay buckeroo. As I recall, there were ten or twelve long maple teeth about fourteen feet long. These were mounted on a frame with only one end of the tooth fastened. The other end was sharpened.

The frame was designed to fit on the front end of the Farmall F-14 tractor. I suspect the 14 meant it had 14 horsepower. It may have at one time, but this tractor was old and not very strong. This tractor had to be cranked by hand to get it started. It was very temperamental and if there was any moisture in the air, the distributor had to be dried out. If you guessed right on how much to choke it for the conditions, it may start. If not, the crankee may have to crank many times. It also had steel wheels. I mean, this tractor wasn't much.

Get the picture of the big comb like affair on the front of the small cantankerous tractor. Finally, it was built and taken to the field which was the closest one we had. For one thing,
~~~~~

it was hard to steer this contraption and secondly, it was too big for the wimpy tractor.

Dad started scooping up the hay. The buckeroo got more and more hay in it. Dad came to the end of the windrow and found he could not turn the tractor with that big load of hay on the buckeroo. He backed up a little and the hay slid off. Dad realigned the tractor so he could pick up the load of hay and be aimed at the barn. Hooray, he got the load to the barn and positioned it under the big hay door. We used slings, so somehow he must have figured a way to get the slings under the load and lift it into the barn.

With great difficulty, he got a few more loads, but he concluded the hay buckeroo was not going to work. Not to worry, he would take these long teeth and they could be the bottom of a two wheeled hay wagon. This meant many trips into the blacksmith shop to fabricate the axles and frame so a wooden rack could be built on it. This was fine with me as I really liked the blacksmith shop.

Most other farmers had four wheeled wagons to haul hay, oat bundles and corn bundles. Not Dad. He could tell several reasons why his two wheeled hay trailer was able to do the same things that the four wheeled rigs did.

THE BEACH

~~~~~

The City of Shell Lake is on the west shore of Shell Lake, the lake. It is a fairly big lake, approximately two miles east to west and two miles north to south. It is nearly round, but it does have a south bay defined by two peninsulas of land. This lake is cold. Later in the summer it may be a little more pleasant, but generally, not so much.

Being young kids, we were attracted to this lake. There was also a nice park at the beach at Shell Lake, the city. Mini-family reunions, 4-H and Church youth groups met there. It was a nice park and in the late 1940s a Shell Lake family donated logs from Oregon to build a very nice shelter. It was large enough to hold large groups of people.

The main attraction is the beach. Of course, you could not go swimming for one hour after eating! There was a large water slide that you better splash water on before you went down it or you would stick and could get burned. There was a dock that went out to where the water was about four feet deep, depending on the water level of the lake.

The beach is nice and sandy both on the shore and in the water. The shallow part was marked off with ropes and floats. There was a drop off and you could find it by walking out further and further. It was at about five to six feet deep. Anchored out in the deep water was the diving raft with a high dive springboard.

I was a fairly good swimmer, but I floated like a rock. By the time I was about ten, I swam out to the diving raft. On a
~~~~~

warm Sunday the raft would be loaded with kids, most were older than me. For most of that year, I was content to dive off the raft, not off the springboard or the steps leading up to it. To be good and truthful, I was a little scared.

The next summer I had made up my mind that I was going to dive off the springboard. I had talked to my Dad and a couple of other older kids and, from what I learned from them, I thought I was ready.

Fairly early in the summer, on a nice Sunday afternoon, the moment of truth had arrived. I swam out to the raft and warmed up with two or three dives off the rungs of the ladder leading up to the diving board. Finally, I decided I was ready and climbed up on to the diving board platform. Gee, the water looked a long way down as it was about ten feet. I let a few kids go ahead, but finally the time had come!

I took a short run, jumped on the end of the springboard and I was off. Try as I might, I could not avoid it. I made a beautiful **belly flop!** I am here to tell you that it really hurt. Man, it nearly knocked the wind out of me and my whole front side just stung. I managed to get back to the diving platform and climbed on. I not only hurt, but I was embarrassed - big time. I recognized a few kids, but tried not looking anyone in the eye. I had to regroup and let the pain go away. I was trying to get my courage up to try again. I came to realize that the spring in the spring board flipped me more than I had anticipated. After all, I had dived off the next to the top rung on the ladder, the rung didn't move, but the springboard did. I thought I had it figured out.

After a half hour or more, I decided the time had come to do the dive again. I was confident! Up the steps I went. Boy, it looks like a long way down. Oh, well, here goes. I took the short run, jumped on the end of the springboard and I was off. Oh, NO!! It was an exact replica of the first belly flop. When I recovered, my next move was to swim toward shore and get away from that springboard. Eventually, I would swim out to the diving raft and dive off the lower springboard and the sides, but I never tried the high dive again.

In the early 1940s, free movies were shown at the beach on Friday or Saturday nights. Many rows of benches were built. The shows started at dusk, so it was late by the time the movie was finished. I had a difficult time staying awake for the entire movie.

There also was a beach access on the north side of the lake. This beach was rocky and not much fun and the water was just as cold. We did swim there many times after making hay on a hot day.

We would see 'dead heads' floating out in the lake. Dad said they were logs that had laid on the bottom of the lake and now were just able to float and only one end would show at the surface of the water. The Shell Lake Lumber Company had a huge sawmill and planing mill on the northwest side of the lake at Shell Lake.

In the winter, pine logs were hauled on to a trestle crossing the south bay via a narrow gauge railroad out on to the ice to make room for more logs. At its peak, about half of the lake would be full of logs when the ice melted. A steam boat 'boomed' the logs over to the saw mill to be processed. This was done by using boom logs that were chained together and the boom rounded up a bunch of logs within the circle. Some of these logs sank and there very likely are some logs down at the bottom today. These logs are valuable and have a distinctive grain because of the long time under water. The wood is called 'water wood'. Several hundred men worked at the Shell Lake Lumber Company. It started in 1881 and closed about 1903. The Shell Lake Boat Company started up using some of the lumber company buildings. The lumber company kept their horses and other livestock in the company pasture. Somehow that land ended up belonging to the Shell Lake School District. About 1954 and 1955 the Shell Lake High School students planted many thousands of Norway pine on the company pasture and other property near the high school. Today that beautiful forest has been thinned once and some trees are up to 60 feet tall, or more.

In the 1940s, some kind of summertime water festival was held at the park. I remember one event was the greased pole climb. Someone cut an aspen tree and peeled it. This made it slippery, but they also smeared lard on the pole. The pole was put in a hole on the edge of the water and it leaned out over the water. There was a five dollar bill attached to the top of the pole. Kids were encouraged to enter and I think only boys did. It was for kids a little older than me, but persons older than high school age were not eligible.

They drew numbers to establish the order that they would climb. There was a time limit for each climber and then they started. There was a huge amount of lard on that pole. The first two or three could only go a short distance, but they rubbed a bunch of lard off the pole. After about ten kids tried, someone thought about putting sand on his body and having sand on his hands. I am pretty sure that kid got the $5.00. I think a lot of moms got the short end of the stick when they washed the clothes with all that lard on them.

Also at the beach was a nice concrete basketball court. I was very interested in that and many hours were spent playing basketball with whomever wanted to play. We did see some pretty good players and during that time period, Shell Lake had a good basketball team for a small town.

BOOKS AND THE RADIO

~~~~~

Going to a small country school we had only a small book shelf with not over a hundred books total. The shelves were marked off so if you were in first grade, you looked for a book from that part of a shelf marked first grade and so on. Most books had copyright dates from in the 1930s or older. I eventually read all the books in that library, even though the school closed after my fourth grade year. I really liked to read at night, especially in the winter. Our teachers would read to all the students and we really enjoyed that.

In the 1940s, I got several books from my maternal Grandfather and Grandmother. They lived in Eau Claire, Wisconsin and were both very interested in books. Two of the books I got from them were written by a Canadian author and both books were about the lives of many different animals and birds. Two of my favorites involved a mountain sheep in the Canadian Rockies and another was about a wolf pack in Texas. I read these stories and others several times.

Jack London's stories were great also. We quite often got books for Christmas and birthdays, so we had a fairly good library at home also. The family that was shipwrecked was an exciting adventure book. Stories about Brer Fox and Brer Rabbit were very enjoyable. All in all, I really liked books. You had to get your imagination going. Since I really liked the woods, any story involving wilderness, animals and adventure were hard for me to pass up. Books from that period of the 1930s and 1940s were quite basic, very little color, but many were great books, nonetheless. There didn't
~~~~~

seem to be many books about football players, baseball players, etc.

Our radio at home was not a floor model, as many people had, but it was quite large and sat on a small table in front of a large mirror. The radio might be on all day with no particular programs to listen to. Noon time, however, was a different story.

Most of the time Mom had lunch ready a little before noon so we could listen to the 'noon time news'. There undoubtedly were soap operas on during the day, but I personally don't know that. Nighttime was different with many interesting programs.

This was before television and quite often after chores were done and supper eaten, we would gather around the radio and listen intently to 'The Inner Sanctum' with its squeaky door, 'Lux Radio Theater', 'Fibber McGee and Molly' and many more. My favorite was 'Sergeant Preston of the Yukon'. It came on at 5:00 p.m. on Sundays. I tried very hard to be home for that program, at least in the winter months.

We visited the Yukon Territory a few years ago and inquired about Sergeant Preston. I was led to believe that I was one of many, many people to inquire about the Sergeant.

During these radio programs, the entire family would be grouped around the radio, deeply engrossed in the unfolding story. All kinds of emotion may be shown, cheers, tears, laughter, smiles, grimaces, body english at times and in general, total involvement in the story line being presented.

My Dad would listen to Badger football games, sometimes. Once in a while I remember of hearing the Green Bay Packers on the air. I remember old time radio with fond memories.

ROUGH AND TUMBLE

~~~~~

My two younger brothers and I had developed a reputation of being wild and rambunctious and, very likely, many more terms were used. We did get a lot out of each day, not unlike other kids that we knew. Most kids, boys especially, are quite active and have so much energy.

I will say that if there was something to climb we probably climbed on it. If there was something to throw, we probably threw it, sometimes at targets that we should not have thrown at. If there was a chance for horseplay, we probably did it. You get the point.

We constantly picked on each other, but we quickly defended each other if any of us were picked on by outsiders, which was very typical of most families. The one story that circulated around the community, I swear, was not true. One brother, not me, had a slingshot that another brother, not me, wanted. Things got hot and the brother wanting the slingshot picked up a piece of lead pipe and hit the other brother over the head with it. The story doesn't say whether he got the sling shot.

When I heard that story, I was up at Oscar's Store and one of the men in the neighborhood was there. He related the story I have told and claimed that he had seen it happen. He continued, "I went home and took a lead pipe and hit a little calf over the head and I know it wasn't half as hard, and it killed the calf, deader than a door nail."

Once again, that did not happen, or at least I don't think so.
~~~~~

Of course, I may not have been there when it happened. That same man claimed he looked over at our new, large barn and saw the Hubin boys running around on the roof. I really can't say that didn't happen. We were rambunctious!

We made sling shots out of a Y shaped branch and strips of rubber cut out of an old inner tube. We needed a little pouch of leather to put the stone in, or whatever we were propelling. We tied the rubber and the pouch on with string. The usual projectiles were stones and we were pretty good shots. Most kids we knew carried a slingshot in their back pocket. You never knew when a good target would present itself.

The very best projectiles were marbles, but we didn't want to part with them. We did search roads, sand pits and other places to get good slingshot rocks. I saw a super-duper sling shot advertised in a comic book. It was round and had four powerful rubber bands. It sounded spectacular, plus it came with a supply of marbles. I ordered it and, when it arrived, it was all it was cracked up to be. There were about 25 marbles with it. It was very accurate and I could shoot farther than with our homemade slingshots.

You always had to be on the look out when you were with other boys with slingshots. You never knew when someone might shoot you in the butt with a rock. Of course, this would call for retaliation and so on and on.

One time in the late 1940s, several of us walked past our bull on the way out to the woods. The bull was lying down, chewing his cud, and without warning, one kid pulled back on his slingshot and drilled the bull right between the eyes. The bull jumped up and now was in a state of 'high pisstification'. He roared and started pawing the ground. We could see that as we looked over our shoulder as we ran to the woods. We never told Dad about that and we stayed away from the bull.

Walking on the railroad tracks was the perfect place to sling-bing. Numerous rocks and a lot of great targets. The glass insulators on the telegraph lines made good targets, too. We rarely broke an insulator, but we could tell if we hit one as it would bing. Later, when taconite, which is a form of iron ore, was made and there were taconite pellets laying along the railroad track, I thought they would be the ultimate slingshot projectile, round and very dense. By that time, I was grown up and had long since given up on using a slingshot.

Talking about comic books, I saw an atomic bomb ring advertised. This was after the two atomic bombs were dropped in Japan to end the war with Japan. I ordered it and it came. It was a bomb mounted on a ring. If you took off the back part of the bomb and looked into it, you saw little flashing lights. Pretty cool! Eventually, I managed to break the band that held the bomb on the ring. I still have the bomb in my can of 'kid junk' and it still flashes little lights, when you take the end off and look in. I don't have a clue how it works. Maybe it really is atomic.

We did make our own kites and would fly them, sometimes. We made them by splitting thin boards from apple crates into narrow sticks. These would be tied or taped in the shape of the outline of an ice cream cone with a triangular hat on top. Next, we cut newspaper to the shape of the kite frame. We mixed up good old reliable flour paste and glued the paper to the frame. The tail was made by taking a short length of string and tying little bits of cloth at small intervals on the string. This was very critical toward having a kite that would fly well. You definitely needed a long string. In those days, stores wrapped things up in packages and wrapped them with string. So, if you were on the ball you saved the string for just this time.

Kite flying was done when things were muddy and windy, like in March or April. Off we would go to a small hill near home. We got the kite launched by holding it in one hand and running into the wind with it until it lifted out of your hand. With any luck you could begin playing out string very carefully and the kite would fly. Many times, however, our engineering skills resulted in temporary failure. Then it was back to tinker with the tail, etc. and try to get it flying.

I never claimed to be a great kite flyer, although I had fairly good luck. I could make paper airplanes, like we all did, but I fell into the middle of the pack on that endeavor.

We figured out how to make parachutes by taking a bandana handkerchief, tying string on all four corners and then tie those ends to a bone from of a piece of round steak. We rolled the whole thing up and threw it in the air. It acted like a parachute and floated down.

Other things that fascinated us were thin little boards called lath. These were found in snow fence and we quickly found they were good for sword fighting, though very hard on the knuckles. We also would grab the lath in the middle and throw it by letting it roll off your fingers and you had to duck your head. This made the coolest buzzing sound. The harder you threw, the louder the buzz.

Maybe we were little hellions as some folks might have thought. We were not mean spirited and we didn't think we were hurting anybody with our antics. Oops. I forgot Mom and Dad. They must have really been disappointed in our behavior then.

But, "It is your turn to wipe the dishes!" "It is yours!" "Want to draw straws!" "Two out of three!" And on and on.

LIGHTNING

~~~~~

Dad built the barn in 1942 and before we could install lightning rods, lightning struck the barn. It blew a hole in the roof right by the haymow light. The wire leading up to the light got fried also. Looking at the hole, it looked like the lightning went out from the barn. Later, I learned that it happens that way even though the lightning clearly is in the sky.

Anyway, Dad got busy and prepared to put up the lightning rods and fix the roof. He had made a little scaffold affair that could be pulled up and down the roof to fasten the lightning rod cables at each location. He got up on the round roof by leaning a long ladder up. He could step off the ladder by using a rope thrown over the top of the roof and attached it to our 1937 Ford car bumper, so he could walk up to the peak.

My oldest brother manned the rope on the car bumper. He had to move the car from time to time. Also used at that time was the moveable scaffold as Dad had to fasten the heavy braided copper ground wire for each of the eight lightning rods. This event took all afternoon, but at last, the lightning rods were attached and hooked up to the ground rods, and the roof was patched. Eventually the lights and wires in the haymow were fixed, too.

This barn was very high and there were no trees near by. Big storms would come along and that barn was the tallest thing around so it became a target for lightning.
~~~~~

If the lightning rod does its job, it will neutralize the barn that the rods are on. This means electricity will stream off the tip of the lightning rod and neutralize the approaching cloud. When this happens at a fast rate, the lightning rod will glow with a bluish-purple light. Many times I saw this ghostly light on the top of the barn. It was beautiful, but scary. The barn never did get struck by lightning again.

I remember seeing blue balls, apparently of electricity, come right out of an electrical outlet in the house when a big storm was near. Once I saw one shoot out of the television. These are examples of ball lightning and are not supposed to be dangerous. Sometimes they would occur so fast you weren't even sure you saw them. I have heard of people seeing the balls roll along overhead electric wires. Some even float down out of the sky during a storm. Pretty scary stuff.

THE WHEELCHAIR

~~~~~

My paternal Grandma was a kindly, wonderful lady who, by the time I knew her in the 1940s, was getting quite frail. She had raised thirteen children and she was tired. Also, she had fallen and broken one of her hips in the early 1940s so she rode in a wheelchair. In those days, surgeons could not pin hip bones like they do now. My Grandpa had died in 1942, so she was alone.

All of this was before Medicare. Since she and Grandpa had lost their farm in the depression, they had very little in savings, like probably no savings at all. Her only way to have a place to stay was to spend time with her children who could have her. This poor lady had to be packed up and moved from place to place. She could stay for a few weeks at a time, at least that is what she did at our place. This meant she had to get used to a new routine in each home. With three rambunctious boys, her time at our house probably raised her anxiety level.

Grandma loved to work. In fact, she said she was not happy unless she could work. Wow. As a small kid who basically disliked work, that was hard for me to understand. She really liked going outside and looking at the flowers and the yard. Her wheelchair was sure hard to push on the lawn.

My brothers and I were fascinated with that wheelchair. Boy, that would be cool to get in and spin around and do other things. Eventually, we realized that Grandma went to bed fairly early, so maybe we could sneak in to her bedroom and borrow the wheelchair for a few minutes. Finally we
~~~~~

got the chance and were able to take the wheelchair into our living room. We were quiet and took turns. Boy, it was fun to spin around. We sneaked the wheelchair back into her bedroom and hoped we could do it again. Nothing was said about using her chair the next day. I do not know where Mom and Dad were as I know they would have put the kibosh on our idea.

A few nights later, we had the same opportunity to use the chair. We sneaked in to the bedroom and drats! Grandma had tied her chair to the bed post. Enough said.

She really was a very nice lady. One day she asked if we could help find her glasses. She said she had them a few minutes ago. We looked and looked. Then one of us noticed that she had put them up on her hair. She was embarrassed.

She could shell peas in a flash. In those days, we darned holes in the socks and she showed each of us boys how to do it. She mended any clothes that needed patches. It was very hard for her to just sit and not have something to do. After several weeks, she moved to stay with one of her daughters and I think she passed away while she was living there.

When I think about how Grandma worked in her long life, I am amazed. She was a wonderful lady.

Many people who lived in Grandma's early days had no electricity, water was pumped by hand and carried into the house, or wherever it was needed, and if warm water was wanted, it was heated on a wood stove. Cooking was done with the wood stove, as well as all the baking and ironing clothes was done with flat irons heated on that same stove. The outhouse was the forerunner of indoor plumbing and bathrooms. Light was from kerosene lanterns and candles. Travel was by horse, horse and buggy or walking. Train travel was very important.

We can be proud of how much progress has been made with care for the elderly or handicapped. Today, Grandma would have been able to maneuver her wheelchair through self-opening doors, up ramps and in general find life a little easier. Home health care, assisted living and much improved medical procedures are great improvements. Life is still hard for the elderly and physically handicapped, but it is way better that it was in Grandma's day.

SUMMER CELEBRATIONS

~~~~~

Shell Lake has a small airport and it was opened about 1947. There may have been a dirt air strip before, that I do not know. Anyway, the big day for the airport grand opening arrived and my folks took the three of us boys in town to take part in the celebration. Some speakers said a few words and then airplane rides were given to anyone wanting to take a ride. I think a small fee was charged, but we did not get a ride that day.

Most of the airplanes seemed to be small, some were tail draggers. As the afternoon wore on games were played, including bingo. I sat by Mom and we played. One of the bingo cards I had was a winner and I won a meat carving set. Two long knives and large fork. I was impressed.

There was a very large crowd and late in the afternoon, a plane took off and promptly fell into the underbrush at the end of the runway, which in those days, as I recall, ran north and south. Immediately, several men ran to see what happened and to help out. I recall they were able to push the plane out of the brush and back on the runway. No one was hurt. Today, the runway runs northwest to southeast.

Another summer celebration my parents and we three boys attended was at Hayward, Wisconsin. A world record musky was caught near Hayward and this was the first Musky Festival. It was in the late 1940s. The Musky Festival is still going on after all these years.

The ceremony didn't draw a huge crowd as I recall, however,
~~~~~

maybe we didn't see all of the activities. We did see the world record musky up close. It weighed about 65 pounds and was huge. A guy by the name of Spay caught it. He later caught two more new world record musky near Hayward, including the current world record of a little over 69 pounds.

There is an Agricultural Research Station just east of Spooner. It is run by the University of Wisconsin Extension and does extensive research on various crops. Today, it is an outstanding sheep farm also. When the mother sheep, called ewes, have babies, the little lambs are put on milk replacer and the ewes are milked. There is a milking parlor and sheep milk is in high demand. Currently the milk sells for about seven times the price of cow's milk.

Back in the late 1940s, I don't recall if there were sheep or not. I do know that they raised a wide range of crops and several varieties of each one. Since it was an experimental farm, professors from the University of Wisconsin oversaw the test plots.

Each summer the farm held Field Days. This was a big event as there were huge numbers of farmers in northwest Wisconsin. At that time, Dad was an agriculture teacher and was very interested in all the research that went on there. He would take us boys and we would ride on wagons, pulled by tractors, and tour the entire farm. Stops were made to explain what was happening with the various plots.

Somehow, I got separated from Dad and my brothers and when my wagon got back to where Dad's car was parked, it was gone. Now what? It was getting late and I figured Dad had to get home and do chores. I thought I'd better start walking. It was about six miles right down U. S. Highway 53. But first I had to walk through part of the city of Spooner.

I started walking and it was not long before I could see five or six boys in a yard near the road I was on. I walked by and as I did they started yelling at me. They wanted to know if I wanted to fight. I kept my mouth shut and kept walking and they left me alone. My knees would have been knocking if I had been standing still.

Finally, I was out of town and heading south on U. S. Highway 53. I was about halfway home when Dad came along and picked me up. I sure was happy to see him. He apologized, but said he had to get the cows milked. Oh, well - it turned out alright, but those boys in Spooner sure scared me. I did not want to walk past there ever again.

This past summer the Agricultural Research Station celebrated 100 years of operation.

HI! HOW ARE YOU?

~~~~~

That is what the chanting Indians sounded like to me as they performed on Friday or Saturday nights in Spooner. These colorful Indians were from the Chippewa Tribe by Hayward. The performances were held on a grassy area just southwest of the train depot in Spooner. Today this area is a parking lot.

This was a big deal during the summer months in the 1940s. Huge crowds attended to watch and listen to them. There was a constant steady drum beat by several drummers beating on a single large drum.

There were many performers of all ages, both male and female. The costumes were generally very colorful and most had many feathers. Their shirts, jackets and dresses had very elaborate bead or quill patterns on them.

The program started and various groups would dance. This included some very young children about four to five years old. One dance I remember was the 'hoop dance' performed by young boys approximately 10 years old. The dancers came out with a wooden hoop about twenty inches in diameter. As they danced they stepped through the hoop, passed it from one arm to the other by ducking their head through it. They passed the hoop the entire length of their bodies.

There were several young boys doing the 'hoop dance' at the same time. They gave out war whoops and chanted as they danced. Without a doubt, it was my favorite part of the show. These young Indian boys with their black hair
~~~~~

and flashing black eyes were impressive. They were very enthusiastic.

Returning home, I got the idea of using an inner tube to see if I could do some of the ‘hoop dance’ stunts. I found out that I could. I thought, maybe it wasn’t quite as hard as it looked.

In our bookcase of library books at the Beaver Brook School were several books about Indians. I read them enthusiastically. I was fascinated that they could live in a teepee or other shelter in the woods, on the plains or in the mountains. They had to find their food and they did grow some. We grew some, but we got other food from the store. The Indians, in my books, had no stores.

About this time, our teacher read *‘The Song of Hiawatha’* by Longfellow, to us at school. That was a wonderful poem. What she read to us was the short version. I inherited a book my maternal Grandfather received from his Sunday School Class in 1901 in Eau Claire, Wisconsin. The cover was made of seal skin. This book was published in 1893 and *‘The Song of Hiawatha’* is 115 pages long! Far longer that the short version we are familiar with.

LITTLE LEAGUE

~~~~~

There weren't any organized sports around our neighborhood in the 1940s. We did play a fair amount of ball, however. While at the Beaver Brook School, we had county softball tournaments up at Spooner. All the kids in our school played, from first grade to eighth grade. In the spring we played 'work up' softball at recess, noon and maybe even before school. That was the end of the organization. We played softball at recess and noon while attending Shell Lake Grade School. There were tournaments for bigger schools up at Spooner. We didn't play against the country schools because of the huge difference in the number of students attending.

I did not play baseball until in high school. Most of us had baseballs as well as softballs, but we did not have a baseball field to play on until we got to high school. Playing catch with a friend was done frequently in spring and summer. Many games were played on improvised fields. The bases were made from whatever was handy, a piece of board, cardboard, or someone's shirt. Much discussion took place concerning ground rules.

Other than getting a team organized for the county tournament, there were no adults coaching or umpiring. We organized our own games, mostly at school. Our 4-H club did play one or two other clubs on occasion. This was for both boys and girls.

In the fall, we played football, both touch and tackle. This was organized by the kids and it could be rough. 'Give me
~~~~~

the ball and I will plow' was a common expression. A person could get some injuries and for sure, you got dirty. Sitting in the classroom with a grass-stained clothes smell was not pleasant.

Most basketball we played was unsupervised. Noon hour in the gym was hectic. There were many basketballs bouncing, flying around and kids going helter skelter. But we loved it.

We did have organized basketball beginning in 6th grade. That was a program called 'The Midgets' and we had a coach. We met after school when the high school team had a game, because the gym was available on game days. Nearly every boy tried out and no one was cut. We learned some drills, learned about team work and defense. Learning the rules was high on the list and boy it was fun to play. Most of us really enjoyed shooting baskets and many kids had a basket at home as well as a basketball. We played a few games against midgets from other towns. That was exciting and we really enjoyed playing against another team. The games were played helter skelter and appeared to be unorganized. It was fun and it was a start.

We had a basket hanging on the east side of the barn, or in the east end of the haymow after the hay was out. I really enjoyed shooting baskets. I was amazed how big the basket was in comparison to the ball when we got our first basket. Many hours were spent shooting and very little time spent dribbling because of the uneven ground. Kids of my era were good shots. However, we were not good dribblers and ball handlers. We could pass pretty well, however.

THE PIANO

~~~~~~

In the sixth grade, my Mother signed me up for piano lessons. This should be cool, I thought, because I could get out of school for one hour each week. And it was cool, until I got the first lesson. My teacher must have taken one look at me and figured this was a lost cause. I would have to admit she was probably right.

We started in with the first lesson. It must have gone something like this. This is a piano and these are the keys. Any questions? Well, yes, I had many questions, like what am I doing here? I think we instinctively did not like each other from the first time she opened her door and saw me.

Somehow, we got through that lesson and I happily went back to school. That night Mom asked me how the piano lesson went. I didn't lie so I told her, "I thought I was going to throw up. That piano lesson was the worst thing I have ever done." Of course, I had not been to the dentist yet. Mom said, "Peter, get used to it because you are not going to quit." I could tell Mom thought the time had come to try to polish this rough edged kid a little and she was determined. I could see it in her eyes.

Each week I dreaded the approach of the piano lesson. I did practice and I got a little better. When the dreaded hour arrived, I began to trudge the six blocks to my piano lesson.

Spring rolled around and the piano teacher announced that there would be a recital in a few weeks. Every student had
~~~~~~

to play at least one song. I wondered if she would let me play chop sticks. That one I could handle.

Betty was a cute girl in my class at school and she took lessons from the same teacher. She could really play. What amazed me was how people could learn to use all ten fingers and thumbs and do it so fast. That was Betty and other more advanced students.

The teacher got me going on a song that sounded like an Indian war dance. It lasted about thirty seconds and, believe it or not, I could play it. Never mind that it was by far the simplest song on the recital. At least I got through it and Mom and Dad didn't seem too upset.

Summer came and after the recital, thankfully, there were no more lessons until school started in the fall. Fall rolled around and school started and I lobbied hard, but to no avail. "You will take piano lessons, for at least this coming year," my Mom said. If I could get through this year, it sounded like I might be off the hook. I certainly hoped so.

Lessons started and I was still in Book Number One. I had grown a little so I really felt stupid still trying to get out of that book. Things were not any better between the piano teacher and me. Many days I got the feeling that I was wasting her time as well as mine.

Finally, the dreaded announcement. There will be a recital in a few weeks. I did not even dread that thought. I really felt that when I got through with that, I would be allowed to quit piano lessons. I redoubled my efforts. I could see the light at the end of the tunnel.

The day of the recital arrived and there were several kids still in Book Number One. Of course, they were in second and third grade.

I don't even remember what I played. It probably lasted about a minute and then I was done. I went into the summer smug in my thinking that I was done with piano. I made up my mind to wait until school was ready to start to plead my case to Mom.

The end of the summer came and Mom told me, "You won't have to take piano lessons unless you want to." Sorry Mom, but no thanks. I did thank her for trying to help me.

About seventh grade we were encouraged to try out for the junior band. The music teacher got me started on the clarinet. I guess you can figure out how that went. Too many fingers to teach to play. I did ask about the Tuba. It only has three valves so I thought teaching three fingers to play should be better than ten. Besides, I was getting fairly large so maybe I should carry a big tuba instead of a little clarinet.

I really liked playing the tuba and did so all through high school. We had vocal music class in grade school and I enjoyed singing. I think that most kids seemed to. I really enjoyed it because there were no fingers to have to train. In high school, I was part of a boys quartet. Later we were joined by four girls and became an octet. Remember that Betty that played the piano so well? She was one of these girls. A few years later we were married and still are today.

LITTLE CRITTERS

~~~~~~

On my way to the reservoir one day in the 1940s, I walked through our neighbor's pasture. There was a lone Norway pine that I walked near. I noticed a bird sitting on the lowest limb of that tree. I walked closer and saw it was an owl, a very small owl, only about six inches high. I could see that it had a dead mouse under one of its feet.

It let me walk to within three feet of it. It looked at me with half opened eyes and was about even with my face. It was the neatest thing to see. It didn't seem to mind me standing so close to it. I watched for ten to fifteen minutes and from time to time it swiveled its head to look around.

I wondered if there was something wrong with this little owl. I slowly reached up and touched his foot without the mouse. Away it flew, mouse and all. There was nothing wrong with it. When I got home, I got the bird book out and found it was a saw-whet owl. It was full grown and they are known to let people approach them. I could certainly attest to that fact. The encounter with that little owl is one of my fondest memories of my animal friends.

Another fond memory occurred during Christmas vacation about two years later. My brothers and I were cutting logs out of some trees my Dad had bulldozed out to clear land for a new field. The trees had been pushed off to the edge of the field the summer before. We were using a two man crosscut saw and were struggling with it. We were not very good sawyers.
~~~~~~

I moved a branch one day and under it was a little dark mouse-like critter. It sat on its haunches and looked at me with its mouth open. It couldn't have been over two and one half inches long. It stayed in the same place so I reached down to see if I could catch it. It caught me!!! When my hand was about six inches away, the little bugger jumped up and bit my glove in the web between my thumb and hand. It would not let go. I showed my brothers. I shook my glove. It still hung on. This went on for several minutes. I tried prying if off with a stick and after several tries, it let go and fell into the snow. It did not run away but sat on its haunches with its mouth open, ready to attack again. We left it and admired its spunk.

We had just come into contact with a shrew, probably the toughest animal for its size that there is. They have teeth like a dog, so they are not closely related to mice. They have tremendous appetites and need to eat more than their weight each day. They live on bugs, worms and insects that live just under the leaves in a forest. They will also attack and kill mice much bigger than themselves.

In later years, I have seen shrews running in the leaves. They make a high pitched bird like sound as they run. Over the years, we have had cats that would catch shrews and leave them on our door step. It is as if to say, "There, I killed this mean little shrew." For whatever reason, our cats would not eat shrews.

I also saw a least weasel several times. They are about six inches long with their tail and they turn white in winter, except for the tip of their tail and the tip of its ears. In this stage, the fur pelt is called ermine.

On two occasions, I saw one of these little weasels carrying a mouse with its head thrown back to avoid stepping on the mouse as it ran.

One evening, just as it was getting dark, I had gone for a walk in our woods. I walked near a thick grove of trees and all of a sudden five great horned owls flew out and went over my head. One must have hit a branch because it fell to the ground near me. These large owls were nearly full grown and are impressive. They stand around twenty inches high or more.

This youngster seemed dazed so I moved closer and he started snapping his beak at me. He flapped his wings also and I got the idea he may be injured and I should try to take it home to let it recover. I moved in closer and as it flapped its wing I managed to grab the tip of one wing. It kept flapping the other wing and I was able to grab the tip of it also. By holding both tips in one hand I could carry it, so I headed for home. I was amazed how light this big bird was. It continued snapping its beak all the way home.

I showed the owl to Dad. He thought it had just been dazed. We put it down on the lawn and it just sat there looking at us with its big yellow eyes. It stopped snapping its beak. After about two minutes this big owl just took off without a sound. What an impressive bird. I was so happy it appeared to be alright.

BUS RIDES

~~~~~~

When the Beaver Brook School closed in 1948, I had finished grade four. Grade five was at Shell Lake and that meant I had to ride the school bus. This was all new to me.

My parents found out about what time the bus would be going past our house and where we would have to be to meet it. That year we had to walk up to U. S. Highway 53 and the bus would pick us up there.

One of my brothers was in third grade and the other one was in first grade. Our Mom went with us that first morning. Along came the big bus. It was red, white and blue striped with white window panels. It did not have a number on it.

The bus stopped and on we went. The bus was more than half-full with other students, but there was an empty seat and we all climbed into it. We were scared! I did recognize two or three kids from our old school and that helped. The driver was a kindly old gentleman and seemed friendly. We continued on picking up more kids.

The year before, the Beaver Brook School Board had voted to close and because of our location it was possible for parents of students in the Beaver Brook School District to choose what school district they could send the grades one through eight students to.

Meetings were held and the principals of Shell Lake and Spooner districts made their pitch to the parents and school
~~~~~~

board. A big factor was what school district your immediate neighbors belonged to. In other words, if all your neighbors property around you belonged to the Shell Lake district, you had to also. No isolated islands were allowed.

Anyway, that had all been worked out and about half of the kids went to Shell Lake and the other half went to Spooner to school.

For the first time in my school career, I was around high school students as they rode the bus, too. Boy, some of them sure seemed big to a lowly fifth grader. Finally, we arrived at school. Mom and Dad had driven in to school and were waiting to take us to our proper rooms and meet the teachers. Other buses were arriving and they were red, white and blue striped, also. Our bus, however, had the white window frames. I had to remember that in order to get a ride home.

One of the kids we picked up was Betty. I remembered her from picking beans. She was a fifth grader also and she was cute. Mom and Dad took us to our rooms. Wow, one class of all fifth graders. That was a new experience for me. One of my old classmates, Bonnie, was in the fifth grade so I was not completely alone. Gary, my other Beaver Brook schoolmate the year before, apparently went to Spooner.

Our new class was fun. About twenty-seven students all in fifth grade and for lunch we went to the lunchroom and ate 'hot lunch'. No more lunch bucket meals. Even though at times I preferred Mom's meals to the hot lunch meals. One meal Mom made was grated carrot sandwiches. I liked them. Most meals on the hot lunch program were fine, but . . . . once in awhile . . . . not so good.

The afternoon part of the day got finished and we were dismissed to go home. What confusion as all these many, many kids were excused at one time. It seemed like a mob! Many of us were headed for the buses.

Ah-ha, there was the bus with the white window frames. Yes, the same kindly old man was driving. I looked for my brothers and, low and behold, Mom and Dad were there to be sure they got on the bus alright. We wanted to ride home with them, but they said, "No, we will see you at home." That was nice for my brothers. They were only in first and third grade, and I was a big fifth grader and didn't need my Mom and Dad to get me on the bus! It was sure nice to see them, however.

The bus got filled up and off we went. We went to roads southeast of Shell Lake and dropped off kids. Many of the kids lived in West Sarona. Finally, we headed toward home and our stop. Off we went and ran the eighth of a mile home. Boy, that was an exciting day. When I stop to think of it, there were probably as many new things to get used to that day than any day in my life. Getting started in a new school can be very stressful on kids, especially if they don't know anyone at school to help get them acclimated.

Riding the bus was an eye opener. From first graders to seniors in high school and every age in between. In those days, no students had their own car to drive to school. Once in a great while, some of the students might be able to drive their parent's car to school, but nothing like we see at our schools today.

Generally, everyone looked out for the little ones. Students in grade five and above found life could get complicated. Older kids may chase you out of a seat and, if you resisted, they threw you out of the seat. A lot of good natured ribbing went on. Sometimes not so good natured. Some fighting occurred and when that happened, the driver stopped the bus and reprimanded those involved. That usually meant sitting in a front seat for several days. I served time in the front seat on occasion.

The bus would be full when we left school at the end of the day as well as when we arrived at school in the morning. The smaller kids usually sat three to a seat. As bus riders, we were often called on to push to get the bus out of snow banks or mud. We did not think much about it. Some snow banks were plowed up so they were higher than the bus. In the 1940s we had tons of snow. The heaters in the back of the bus did not put out much heat in really cold weather so we could get cold on our ride to or from school.

Nearly every year the bus route would be different to pick up all the kids. Most times the bus picked us up at the end of our driveway. Many years we could see the bus approach from a distance. This meant that in the winter one brother would be on the look out for the bus. 'Here it comes' caused a flurry of activity as we ran off to get on the bus.

When I started high school, I went out for football. Practice was held the last two periods of the day because many of us rode the bus. It was a real struggle to shower and put on some clothes and catch the bus after practice. I generally ran out carrying my shirt and hoping the bus had not left.

Many times, if the buses had only gone a block or so, they would stop when other kids would see us trying to get to them. I was not alone.

On a few occasions, the bus had gone too far, but I could hustle my buns down across the football field in the hollow, cross on a swampy path and up a steep hill and hopefully catch the bus. This was about a quarter of a mile and if the bus had to wait for traffic at the stop sign, I could make it. More than once I just missed it so that meant walking the four and one-half miles home. Sometimes, neighbors might pick me up. Other years the bus went south out of town, so that was not an option, and I began walking.

Many years I would save a seat for my classmate, Betty. She sure was smart and cute, also.

EGGS

~~~~~

In the 1940s, my parents had chickens, like nearly everyone in our neighborhood did. Some were raised to be eaten as fryers, others were for producing eggs and were called hens. Those breeds were not as 'meaty' as the breeds raised for fryers. When hens reached the end of their productive life, they were processed and became 'stewing hens'. I think they ended up in soup.

Eggs were gathered daily and if more were gathered than were eaten, the excess eggs were cleaned and crated to be sold to the grocery store. Some people stopped at the farm to buy fresh eggs, also.

Hens naturally 'set' on their eggs after they laid them. Apparently this is an inborn instinct to hatch the egg into a baby chick. With no rooster around, our hens 'setting' on their eggs was an exercise in futility.

One day my two brothers and I discovered a 'clutch' of twenty-one eggs under a bush near the chicken coop. Apparently one hen had selected this spot to raise her brood. We could tell the eggs had been there for some time. We broke one egg and boy did it ever **stink!** Rotten egg smell is terrible. Someone got the bright idea of a rotten egg fight. We agreed to divide up the eggs and not throw any until war could be declared. We got pails and each got their allotment of rotten eggs. We separated by about 25 feet and war was declared.

As I recall, the first egg I threw broke from the force of
~~~~~

throwing it. That meant my hand was full of rotten egg. That was **awful!** Talk about slimy, stinky stuff. About that time, eggs came flying at me from my brothers. Even if they didn't hit you, they broke near by and fouled up the air.

The battle combatants were on the move. I ran down one brother and fired an egg on to his back. Another brother moved in on me and I got hit somewhere. I retaliated and went after that brother.

This went on for a few minutes, but it wasn't long before we were out of rotten eggs. We still had a score to settle so we took a few fresh eggs and continued. Finally, Mom saw what we were doing and put the kibosh on our fun. Clean up came next.

ODDS AND ENDS

~~~~~

One afternoon, just after leaving the Beaver Brook School, I could hear some tapping in a large basswood tree in Norton's yard. On the other side of the tree was a big pile of wood chips. About that time, a bird stuck its head out of the hole it was making at the base of the tree. It was a huge woodpecker. It dug the chips away and came out of the hole and scratched the chips away from the tree.

The bird was about the size of a crow and I had never seen one before. It was a pileated woodpecker. Anyway, up inside of the tree it went. Bang - bang - bang more chips fell. Down it came, dug out the chips, looked around and back up and pecked some more chips. It was a fascinating sight and I watched it for a long time.

* * * * * * * * * *

My brothers and I had been given a couple of bow and arrow sets for Christmas one year in the late 1940s. We quickly lost the few arrows that came with the bows. Our solution was to take relatively straight willow branches, peel them, cut a notch in one end and tape a 16 penny nail on the other end. We would cut the head off the nail before taping it on our 'arrow'.

The bows were simple wooden bows, not recurved. The compound bow had not been invented. We shot at a lot of different targets and lost a lot of arrows. We were lousy shots, but if we were close enough we might hit something.
~~~~~

One thing we did was shoot an arrow straight up to see how close you could get to where it landed. WOW. Ones that came straight down were nearly impossible to tell if it would hit you.

* * * * * * * * * *

One morning, I got the bright idea of shooting a cow with my bow and arrow, as they came out of the barn after being milked. I plugged a cow in the neck and about that time Dad was following the cows out. He was hot!! He told me to not come home until I got that arrow out of the cow.

The cow took off and I was hot on her tail. We covered much of the pasture and after about an hour the cow went through some brush and the arrow fell out. Talk about a stupid trick.

* * * * * * * * * *

My oldest brother lost his senior class ring one winter day in about 1947 while out spreading manure. He had it in his pocket and leaned down to do something with the old F-14 tractor and he surmised that is when it fell out.

When the snow melted the following spring, we went looking for it. We had no luck. About the following spring, I was out pretending to be an Indian sneaking around through the woods and fields trying to make myself hard to be seen. Anyway, I was crossing the field where the ring was lost and a car went by on U. S. Highway 53. I laid flat on the ground so the people in the car would not be able to see me. While I was lying there, waiting for the car to pass, I thought 'this is about where Dave lost his ring'. I looked down and there was the lost ring, about six inches from my face.

I took the ring home and presented it to my brother. I think he rewarded me with fifty cents.

* * * * * * * * * * *

When my friend and I were in seventh grade, we got the idea that we should learn taxidermy. We got some money together and enrolled in the Northwest School of Taxidermy at Omaha, Nebraska.

This was a correspondence type course that you were supposed to learn by reading the pamphlets they sent to you.

They recommended that we start with a bird, like a sparrow. We ordered some .22 bird shot so we could shoot a sparrow without putting a big hole in it. We quickly found out that you better not be over twelve feet from the bird, otherwise the pellets were so small they didn't hurt the bird.

We shot a couple of sparrows, and following the directions, skinned the birds. That may sound easy but, believe me, the skin is easily cut or torn. Skinning the head and legs was nearly impossible.

Next, we had to cure the hide and form a body the same size as the sparrow. We were supposed to use excelsior or cotton. Needless to say, we were complete and total failures. We pleaded our case and got out of the rest of the lessons. Thank goodness.

* * * * * * * * * * *

One summer day, my brothers and I were making 'rock slides' on our neighbors large rock pile. One of my brothers launched a rock from the top of the pile. His aim was lousy and the rock hit me on the side of my head. That made me see stars!!

My brother must have known I would be mad, and I was. Boy, my head really hurt. He was already heading for home and I was right after him. That day, he probably set the record for the quarter mile run, at least in the Town of Beaver Brook.

My brother got home and hid behind Mom. She negotiated a truce and got ice and put it on the knob on the side of my head. Things finally reverted to normal. My head stopped pounding and the knob eventually disappeared.

* * * * * * * * * * *

When I walked home from Beaver Brook School, I sometimes walked part way with a neighbor girl. She was two grades ahead of me and bigger than I was in the third grade. For whatever reason, she picked on me. Sometimes she would push me around. For a long time, I didn't fight back because I was told 'boys don't hit girls'.

Finally, one spring or fall day, she went too far. I retaliated!! I was really mad and I plowed into her. I knocked her down into the ditch and I was right after her. I pounded on her and hollered, "Don't pick on me any more!"

We went on our separate ways toward home. I was really proud of myself! When I got home, I immediately told Mom what I had done. Oh, was she upset. She said the girl's mother would be over to protest. I stuck to my guns. If she comes over I will just tell her mom what she has been doing to me. I was right!!

Well, this girl's Mom never came over, or called, but I was never picked on by her again. We did remain competitive and once in high school I was leading the whole school in magazine sales and, on the last day of the contest, she turned in more sales than I had held back and she beat me by a few dollars.

* * * * * * * * * *

During the summer when I was about ten or eleven, I picked green beans for a neighbor about two miles west of our place. We got paid two cents per pound the first year and three cents per pound the next year.

Mom or Dad would drop me off or I would ride my bike. You needed a pail to put the beans in. This job was lousy! We generally could not start very early because of the dew.

Each picker was assigned a row and away you went. The boss checked on your skills and if beans were missed you had to go back.

There is no position you could pick in for very long, on your knees, sit on the pail, lay down, stand up and bend over and then start all over again. It was better if you could pick near someone so you could visit. One of my classmates came out to pick. She thought beans grew on trees. She earned twelve cents that day. It was enough to go to the movie that night!

Two of the pickers were Betty and Delores - boy, that Betty was cute!

The second year a neighboring family began picking. The family had three boys picking beans. Later, Dick was in my class at Shell Lake and I got to know that family very well.

Their father drove a 'bug', a truck that was modified with a different transmission so it went slower and could go into the woods. I hooked a ride with these guys most of the summer. This was not big money!! I rarely picked a hundred pounds so my bank didn't fill up very fast.

The third year, my brothers and I planted a bean patch of our own. Boy, we were going to be rolling in the dough. Well, it wasn't long before the weeds were as big as the bean plants. We had forgotten about that. Eventually, we did pick the beans. It was just as lousy a job, even if they were our own beans.

We had to get the beans to the Farmers Union in Shell Lake by four o'clock and we got paid each day. Of course, we got docked for large beans, but in the end we each made some money.

* * * * * * * * * *

Potatoes were harvested by hand in those days. A digger raised the spuds out of the ground and left them on top. Pickers came along with bags and filled them up to a hundred pounds per bag.

There was also the Badger Cranberry Marsh about one mile

from our place. In those days the berries were flooded and workers put on hip boots and 'raked' the berries off the vines. These were brought to the sheds where the vines and other things were sorted out.

Many kids missed school during the harvest as this was a way families could earn extra cash. I only helped with the cranberries one day. I never worked on the spuds. My green bean experience was enough for me.

* * * * * * * * * * *

In the late 1940s, we picked many different fruits and berries to make jam and jelly. The biggest effort went into picking blackberries on our property north of U. S. Highway 53. When that road was built in 1938, it left a triangular piece of our farm on the north side of the highway. Also at that time, my parents were offered $600 or they could put a cattle underpass in. They took the $600.

This property had some fields on it but there is about a ten acre thick forest. It was loaded with big blackberry briars. In late summer, Mom took the three of us boys and we battled the briars, bugs and heat. We picked buckets full of berries. We helped sort and clean the berries to be eaten fresh, or for Mom to make into jam and jelly.

We had quite a few gooseberry bushes in our pasture and Mom really liked gooseberry jelly. These berries had little soft thorns on them and it took a long time to fill a small pail. One time, Mom warned me that there was a bee's nest and not to go near it. Guess what I did. She was right and I got stung.

We also picked pin cherries and choke cherries. We never did go pick blueberries although many people did go up north to pick them.

* * * * * * * * * * *

My friend and I had fished in several lakes nearby. Beaver Brook, with its brook trout finally got me interested. My cousin had given me several tips and the guy at the hardware store where I bought my fly rod helped out, too.

The last day of school was only a half day, so I was home by noon. I dug some worms, grabbed my pole and took my bike to Beaver Brook about one and one-half miles away. It was a beautiful June day, really a perfect day for anything.

I started fishing by a log and bingo, a nice eight and one-half inch brook trout grabbed the worm. I continued downstream and had very good luck. The limit then was ten trout and by late afternoon, I had caught and kept nine trout. They ranged from seven inches to nine and one-half inches. I was proud as could be with the batch of trout.

I got home and the sheep shearer was there to shear our sheep. This guy was about three hundred pounds and looked like he could 'pull off your arm and beat you with the bloody end'. He was going to spend the night and that meant eating meals with us.

I had cleaned the trout, leaving the heads on as I was supposed to do. Mom fried them up for supper and we started eating. This big guy got the platter of fish first and promptly took three trout. That left six trout for five of us, provided Mister Big didn't get to them first. Anyway, he picked up the first trout and took a big bite, head and all. He munched it down and took another big bite. Apparently bones were no problem with him. The rest of us took the bones out and ate the fish. Mr. Big had eaten all three of his trout before any of us had finished our one trout. I don't recall who got the last trout, but I have a hunch it was Mr. Big.

* * * * * * * * * * *

In my youth very few stops were made at the root beer stand. The occasions when we were able to partake were greatly appreciated. Kool-Aid was more our speed.

My Mom and Dad hosted a sliding party for the youth of our church. We had a great time and they all returned to our home for hot chocolate and sandwiches.

In the process of getting lunch ready I was helping and Mom asked me to get something out of the cabinet on the south side of the kitchen. I opened the doors, looking for whatever it was Mom wanted. Low and behold, I spotted a gallon jug of root beer, or at least that is what the label on the jar had written on it. Wow - I closed the door and immediately made a mental note to find a way to get a swig of that root beer.

The church kids left and Mom and Dad went out to see them off. Now was my chance. I hustled back in the house, opened the cabinet door, grabbed the jug of root beer, unscrewed the cap and put it up to my mouth for a big swig. **Big surprise!** The root beer was **vinegar.**

Apparently my Mom had bought vinegar in bulk from the grocery store and it was put in a root beer jug. Sure fooled me!

Vinegar has a very distinctive smell and since I did not swallow it and instead spit it into the sink, there was no way out of this one when Mom and Dad came in the house. They both got a huge laugh out of my attempt to sneak a drink of root beer.

* * * * * * * * * * *

Returning from school each day, three boys were ready for something to eat. Bread, butter, peanut butter and jelly plus a glass or two of milk, we would scrounge through the cupboards and refrigerator. Keeping in mind that we had to be careful not to eat something that Mom had planned for a meal. One thing we all liked on occasion was condensed, or evaporated, milk. We opened it with a church key and consumed spoons full of it.

One day I spotted a can that said condensed milk on it and it was in a red can. I opened the can and went to pour it into a spoon. The contents barely came out. I thought the contents must be spoiled so I threw the can in the garbage.

A few days later Mom wanted to know if anyone knew what happened to the **sweetened condensed milk** she had in the cupboard. I said, “Was it in a red can?” “Yes,” she said. I confessed and told her I threw it out thinking it was spoiled. She said the laugh is on you because that is like eating or drinking candy. I felt pretty stupid.

* * * * * * * * * * *

My mother was the most kind, friendly person anyone could meet. She loved me and I loved her but…..I seemed to have excessive energy when I was young. To the point it was great exasperation for my mother. I was not mean spirited, I did not think, but I seemed to be on the edge of doing things I should not have done. With two younger brothers we made a band of boys that seemed to get a lot out of each day.

Invariably, I would be confronted with - "Did you do that?: You know you shouldn't have done that, I warned you."

Next, she would get her hairbrush and put me over her knee and give me a few swats. She always told me that it hurt her more than it hurt me. Today, I know that was true. At the moment though, I really felt that hair brush.

Looking back, my Mother worked very hard to get me to see the error of my ways. I never ever felt anything but great love for my mother and my father. I do wish I had not been such a "rascal" for my mother in my early youth.

* * * * * * * * * *

EPILOGUE

~~~~~

The 1940s, in northwest Wisconsin, was a very interesting place for a young boy. Looking back at events that occurred then, the author has tried to take the reader back into a very different world and life style.

The stories told here are true. World War II dominated the 1940s and it affected everyone's life. Growing up on a farm near a major highway and railroad with several lakes nearby, seemed like a special place to a young, barefoot boy. Attending the same country school as the author's father did with many acres of woods nearby that needed exploring, provides more story fodder.

The intention of this book is to provide the reader with a chuckle now and then. Also to gain an appreciation of life as it was for the author. The author hopes the reader enjoyed taking a peek into his younger life, as he has enjoyed writing it.

The author is a retired Science teacher and football coach. He and his wife of over 53 years, Betty, raise beef cattle and live on a farm near Spooner, Wisconsin, about five miles from his boyhood home.

~~~~~